I Never Danced at the White House

ART BUCHWALD

I Never Danced
at the White House

G. P. Putnam's Sons
New York

Photo on title page by Yoichi R. Okamoto

Fifth Impression

SBN: 399–11212–X
Library of Congress Catalog Card Number: 73–78585

PRINTED IN THE UNITED STATES OF AMERICA

Contents

Contents   11

I Never Danced at the White House

I. WHAT IS A WATERGATE?

NIXON TALKS TO GOD

Recently President Richard Nixon went to Camp David alone, without family or aides. Press Secretary Ron Ziegler denies it, but it has been reliably reported that the President went up the top of the mountain to speak with God.

"God, God, why are you doing this to me?"

"Doing what, Richard?"

"The Watergate, the cover-up, the grand jury hearings, the Senate investigations. Why me, God?"

"Don't blame me, Richard. I gave you my blessing to win the election, but I didn't tell you to steal it."

"God, I've done everything you told me to do. I ended the war. I defeated poverty. I cleaned the air and the water. I defeated crime in the streets. Surely I deserve a break."

"Richard, I tried to warn you that you had sinful people working for you."

"When, God?"

"Just after the Committee to Reelect the President was formed. When I saw the people you had selected to head up the committee, I was shocked. We've got a long file on them up here."

"Why didn't you tell me, God?"

"I tried to, but Ehrlichman and Haldeman wouldn't let me talk to you on the phone. They said they'd give you the message I called."

"They never told me, God."

"It figures. Then I sent you a telegram saying it was urgent that you contact me."

"The only telegrams I read during that period were those in support of my bombing North Vietnam."

"Finally, Richard, I made one last effort. I showed up at a prayer meeting one Sunday at the White House, and after the sermon I came up to you and said there were men among you who would betray you. Do you know what you did, Richard? You introduced me to Pat and then you gave me a ball-point pen."

"I didn't know it was you, God. So many people show up at these prayer meetings. Is that why you're punishing me—because I snubbed you?"

"I'm not punishing you, Richard. But even I can do just so much. If it were merely a simple case of bugging at the Watergate, I could probably fix it. But your administration is involved in the obstruction of justice, the bribing of witnesses, the forging of papers, wiretapping, perjury, and using the mails to defraud."

"Good God, nobody's perfect!"

"I guess that's what the grand jury is saying."

"Look, I've got less than four years in which to go down as the greatest President in the history of the United States. Give me a break."

"You've got to clean house, Richard. Get rid of everyone who has any connection with the scandal. You must make it perfectly clear you were hoodwinked by everyone on your staff. You must show the American people that when it comes to the Presidency, no one is too big to be sacrificed on the altar of expediency."

"God, are you asking for a human sacrifice?"

"It would show your good faith, Richard."

"All right, I'll do it. Will you take Jeb Magruder, Richard Kleindienst and John Dean III?"

"What kind of sacrifice is that?"

"John Mitchell?"

"Keep going."

"Haldeman and Ehrlichman?"

"That's more like it."

"And then, God, if I sacrifice them, will you keep me out of it?"

"Richard, I can't work miracles."

RICHARD THE THIRD (With No Apologies to Shakespeare)

The setting is the palace at Key Biscayne where Richard III has retired to contemplate his next move.

(*Enter the* DUKE OF ZIEGLER.)

ZIEGLER: My Lord. . . .

RICHARD: Good news or bad news that thou com'st in so bluntly?

ZIEGLER: Bad news, my Lord. Dean has fled to Maryland, Magruder sings in Virginia, and the palace guard is confessing in chorus.

RICHARD: Zounds! I cannot tell if to depart in silence or bitterly to speak in gross reproof. Yet so much is my poverty of spirit, so mighty and so many my defects, that I would rather hide me from my greatness. What say the citizens, dear Ziegler?

ZIEGLER: The citizens are mum, my Lord, except for those who would impeach thy motives at the Watergate.

RICHARD: They do me wrong and I will not endure it! Who is it that complains unto the king that I forsooth am stern and love them not? By the Holy Graham, they love his grace but lightly that fill his ears with such dissentious rumors. A plague upon them all!

ZIEGLER: What shall I tell the citizens, my Lord?

RICHARD: Since you will buckle fortune on my back, to bear

her burden, whe'r I will or no, I must have patience to endure the load; but if black scandal or foul-faced reproach attend the sequel of this sordid affair, your mere enforcement shall acquittance me from all the impure blots and stains thereof.

ZIEGLER: I will say, my Lord, you have no comment. (*He exits.*)

(*Enter* BARON EHRLICHMAN *and* BARON HALDEMAN, *guarded by a lieutenant from the tower.*)

EHRLICHMAN: My Lord, we must depart perforce. Farewell.

HALDEMAN: And to that end we wish your Lordship here t' avoid the censures of the carping world.

RICHARD: Well, your imprisonment shall not be long; I will deliver you or else lie for you. Meantime, have patience. Now I'll strive with troubled thoughts to take a nap, lest leaden slumber peise me down tomorrow. Farewell, dear Haldeman and Ehrlichman, you served me well, though you cannot serve me last.

(EHRLICHMAN *and* HALDEMAN *exit.* RICHARD *goes to sleep.*)

(*Enter the* GHOST *of the* EARL OF MUSKIE.)

GHOST OF MUSKIE: Let me sit heavy on thy soul. Think how thou stab'd'st me in the prime of my career, at Manchester and other places too long to mention. Be cheerful, Richard, I shall forget you not.

(*Enter the* GHOST OF MCGOVERN OF DAKOTA.)

GHOST OF MCGOVERN: When I was mortal, by thee my anointed campaign was punched full of deadly holes. Think of me, dear Richard, virtuous and holy, when justice wields its blade. Live and flourish!

(*The* GHOSTS *vanish.* RICHARD *starts out of his dream.*)

RICHARD: Alas, I am a villain. Yet I lie I am not. My conscience hath a thousand several tongues and every tongue brings in a several tale. And every tale condemns me for a villain. Perjury, perjury in the highest degree!

(*Enter the* DUKE OF REBOZO.)

RICHARD: A horse! A horse! My kingdom for a horse!

REBOZO: Withdraw, my Lord. I will help you to a horse.

RICHARD: Slave, I have set my life upon a cast, and I will stand the hazard of the die. I have slain six crises in the past. Today shall be my seventh. A horse! A horse! My kingdom for a horse!

(*Enter a* MESSENGER.)

MESSENGER: My gracious Sovereign. . . .

RICHARD: Out with it! What bad news now?

MESSENGER: The Duchess of Mitchell has called for your head.

RICHARD: Zounds! By the Holy Mother of Our Lord, this plot
has gone too far!

INSPECTOR COLUMBO AT THE WHITE HOUSE

Peter Falk, playing his famous role of Columbo, walked into
the East Room of the White House in his dirty raincoat and
flashed his police card. "Lieutenant Columbo," he said showing
it to President Nixon. "Say, this sure is a nice house you got
here. How much does a place like this cost?"

"I'm having a private party for my staff," the President said
indignantly. "What do you want?"

"Oh, I really apologize," Columbo said. "I didn't mean to
come busting in on a party. Say, is that a real oil painting of
George Washington? It's a fantastic work of art—don't get me
wrong, I don't know anything about painting."

"Will you state your business, Lieutenant?"

"I'm just making some routine inquiries about the Watergate
bugging case. You see, I'm on loan to the Senate investigating
committee from the Los Angeles Police Department. It will
only take a few minutes."

"We have nothing to hide here," the President said. "This is
my assistant, H. R. Haldeman; my legal aide, John Dean III;
my former assistant, Charles Colson; the former Secretary of
Commerce, Maurice Stans; and the former Attorney General,
John Mitchell, and his wife, Martha."

"This is really a great honor," Columbo said. "I never
thought I would get to meet so many important people. Wait till
I tell my wife. She's really going to be bowled over."

"What exactly is it you want to know?" the President asked.

"Oh, yes," Columbo said, taking out his pad and pencil.
"Now let me see."

Martha Mitchell said, "Lieutenant, I'd like to tell you a few things about the Watergate. . . ."

"Martha, will you shut up?" John Mitchell interrupted.

"They're not going to hang this on my John," Martha said.

"Martha!"

"Can I offer you a drink, Lieutenant?" the President asked.

"Just some orange juice if you've got it, Mr. President. I have a bad stomach. You know in this job you never eat properly. Last night I had a tuna fish sandwich on a roll and. . . ."

"Will you get on with it, Lieutenant?" H. R. Haldeman said.

"I'm sorry, where was I? Oh, yes, now about the Watergate. This is just routine, you understand, but where were each of you the night of the break-in?"

"I was watching *Patton*, the President said.

"I was in Mexico City at a bank," Maurice Stans said.

"I was reading FBI files," John Dean III said.

"I was cutting the budget," H. R. Haldeman replied.

"I'll tell you where John was," Martha Mitchell said.

"Martha, clam up," John Mitchell said.

"Well, if I don't tell him, I'll tell United Press," Martha said.

"You see," Columbo said, shutting his notebook, "I knew this would all be a waste of time. I told them no one in the White House knows anything about the Watergate. Say, that is some rug. Do you mind if I take a picture of it to show the folks in Los Angeles?"

Just then the butler came in with Columbo's glass of orange juice.

"Thank you very much," Columbo said to the butler, "I didn't get your name."

"Alphonse, sir."

"Where were you on the night of the break-in, Alphonse?"

"I was polishing the silver."

"You're lying, Alphonse. You were at the Watergate."

"See here, Columbo," the President said, "you're relying on hearsay evidence."

"No, I'm not, Mr. President. This coaster that the orange juice was served on says 'Property of the Watergate Bar and Grill.' "

"My God," said H. R. Haldeman, "the butler did it."

"Why didn't we think of that?" John Dean III said.

"Thank heavens, Columbo, you discovered the culprit," John Mitchell said. "Now we can all sleep tonight."

Martha Mitchell piped, "Wait a minute, Mr. Columbo, there's a lot more to this than you think."

"Dammit, Martha," yelled John Mitchell, "will you keep your big trap shut?"

THE WATERGATE ARRESTS

Nobody knows how many people will eventually be arrested in the Watergate case, but so many people have been implicated that the Justice Department has contingency plans ready when the indictments are finally handed down.

On May 1, 1971, 12,000 people were arrested in Washington, D.C., in an antiwar demonstration. A Justice official told me he didn't expect the Watergate to break this record, but the department wasn't taking any chances.

"Since D.C. jail may not be able to accommodate everyone involved in the Watergate, we've rented the R. F. K. Stadium to handle the overflow. We also have an option on the Coliseum in case the R. F. K. Stadium fills up."

"That's good thinking," I said.

"We also have chartered buses in Washington, Maryland, and Virginia to transport people to the detention centers. During the May Day demonstrations in 1971, we were accused of violating the constitutional rights of the twelve thousand people we picked up, and we don't intend to be criticized for mishandling the Watergate arrests."

"Do you have enough lawyers to defend all the Watergate people?"

"We don't in Washington, but we have three thousand lawyers standing by in Boston, two thousand in New York and four thousand in Chicago. If this is not enough, the President has authority to call up the American Bar Association Reserves.

"We have thirty C-5A transport planes that can fly a division of airborne lawyers to Washington in two hours."

"You've thought of everything," I told the Justice Department official.

"Obviously when you have mass arrests such as we're expecting in the Watergate case, there will be some abuses, but we intend to have Justice Department lawyers spread out in every section of town to see that the rights of the people are protected. The police have been instructed to use as little force as possible and no tear gas unless it is absolutely necessary."

"You seem to be following the guidelines of former Attorney General Mitchell," I suggested.

"Yes, the former Attorney General was very interested in mass arrests, though I'm certain he never thought we would have to use the same guidelines so soon."

"How long do you think it will take to arraign all the people?"

"It's hard to say. If we can get several judges over to R. F. K. Stadium, I wouldn't think anyone would have to be detained for more than forty-eight hours. But if we have to transport them to the federal courthouse, I can't see how we could get everyone processed in less than a week."

"Is it possible that some of the people you pick up in the Watergate case may be innocent and falsely accused?"

"There's always that possibility," the Justice Department official said, "but we're not talking about an ordinary situation now. We're talking about the Watergate. And whenever you have that many citizens involved in anything, innocent people are going to be caught up in the dragnet. How can you ask a policeman to say to someone in the middle of a mass arrest, 'Did you or didn't you have anything to do with the Watergate case and the cover-up?'"

The Justice Department official warned me not to predict the number of people who would eventually be arrested. "I think the newspapers have been overplaying the story," he said. "While we're ready to meet any contingency and handle up to fifteen thousand suspects, our prediction is that no more than five thousand people from the White House and the Committee to Reelect the President will actually be detained."

A BLOW AGAINST CASTRO

The forgotten men of the Watergate Affair are the four Cuban refugees who were among the seven men convicted of bugging the Democratic headquarters on June 17, 1972. To this day, these men think they were hired to strike a blow against Fidel Castro.

At this very moment, they are probably sitting in their Washington, D.C., jail cells discussing how they had contributed to Castro's downfall.

"Well, *amigos,* it will just be a matter of time until we will be back home in Havana."

"That is true, dear friends. Even though we have been caught, Castro must be shaking in his boots, knowing we could get into the Watergate without his stopping us."

"I spoke to G. Gordon Liddy in the mess hall yesterday, and he told me the President is very proud of us for what we did to halt Communism from spreading to South America."

"*Sí,* he told me the same thing. He said if it hadn't been for us Cubans, Fidel would now be sleeping in the Watergate Hotel."

"I must be dumb, *amigos,* but I still don't understand what we were doing in the Democratic National Headquarters."

"*Estúpido!* We were putting in a bug so we could listen in on the Democrats' telephone line to Havana. Mr. Liddy said the Democrats did nothing during the election without first checking with Fidel. It was essential to the Republicans to know what the Democrats were cooking up."

"But who paid us all the money?"

"The Committee to Reelect the President and to Defeat Castro. They had a special espionage fund set aside for this purpose.

"It was in cash because the committee was afraid that if they used checks, Castro would find out about it and abort our revolution."

"But why do we have to keep going in front of the grand jury all the time?"

"You don't know why? Because the Democrats are trying to prove our bugging had nothing to do with Cuba. They say it had to do with the American election."

"*Caramba!* Everyone knows we wouldn't be in on a bugging if it didn't have to do with Cuba. Those Democrats are real crazy people if they think we would be involved in something like this if it wasn't to get Castro."

"I read in the newspaper where high people in the White House were behind the bugging of the Watergate."

"Why shouldn't they be? They hate Fidel as much as we do. Mr. Liddy told me the White House got reports on everything that happened at the Watergate. He said once they got enough information, the President was going to launch an attack at the Bay of Pigs."

"But if the White House approved of what we were doing, why are we still in jail?"

"To lull Castro into a false sense of security. He thinks the Justice Department is mad at us for what we did. Once Castro lets his guard down, they will fly us to southern Florida and let us lead the invasion against the beaches."

"But the judge said we could get up to forty years in jail."

"Mr. Liddy said not to pay any attention to the judge. He was just mad because he thought the bugging had to do with the elections. Once he finds out it was against Castro, he will give us all medals."

"I don't know why I have a bad feeling about all this. There are too many people involved who weren't Cubans. Maybe there was more to it than we know."

"Imbecile! Do you think the highest officials in the President's own party would lie to Cuban refugees?"

"I guess not. But if I had it to do all over again, I would stay in my hacienda in Miami."

THE NEW NEW (SIC) NIXON

We've had an Old Nixon and a New Nixon, and one Monday night on nationwide television we saw a New New Nixon. How the New New Nixon came to be President is a very interesting story.

Back in January, 1972, the New Nixon was engaged in working out the details of the Vietnam cease-fire and solving difficult problems with Red China and the Soviet Union. Because the duties of the Presidency consumed so much of his time, he turned over his reelection campaign to the Old Nixon, who at the time was unemployed and needed the work.

On June 17, while the New Nixon was in Florida resting up from his trip to Moscow, he received word of the Watergate break-in. He was appalled at this senseless, illegal action and was shocked to learn that employees of the Committee to Reelect the President were involved.

The first thing he did was to call the Old Nixon and order an immediate investigation to find out who was responsible.

The Old Nixon promised the President that he would leave no stone unturned in rooting out the people who were involved in this sordid affair.

As the weeks went by, the Washington *Post* and other newspapers started writing that people in the White House were involved in the Watergate. The President called in the Old Nixon and asked him what he knew about it.

The Old Nixon replied, "It is rotten journalism, hearsay and mudslinging at its worst. I have talked to John Dean III, Charles Colson, John Mitchell, Jeb Magruder, H. R. Haldeman, and John Ehrlichman, and they have assured me that no one in a position of any responsibility had anything to do with the Watergate. I also have seen Pat Gray's FBI files and everyone is clean."

The New Nixon breathed a sigh of relief, but he gave further instructions to the Old Nixon. "I don't want a whitewash. The chips must fall where they may."

"Yes, sir."

On March 21 the President received new information implicating members of his own White House family. This information shocked and appalled the New Nixon because the White House was a sacred trust.

He called in the Old Nixon and demanded his resignation.

"I'm not going to be the scapegoat," the Old Nixon shouted.

"If I go, I'm going to involve a lot of other people. This whole Watergate mess wasn't my idea, and I'm going to name names."

The New Nixon told the Old Nixon he could stay on. Then the New Nixon went to Camp David to think about what he should do. He knew he had to get rid of the Old Nixon. However, he was hoping to save Ehrlichman and Haldeman.

But the pressure was too great, and a group of highly influential Republicans flew in secretly to see him. They told him not only would he have to get rid of the Old Nixon, Kleindienst, John Dean III, Ehrlichman and Haldeman, but he would also have to go himself.

The New Nixon couldn't believe it. "I haven't been accused of anything."

One of the Republican leaders said, "In matters as sensitive as guarding the integrity of our democratic process, it is essential that the public have total confidence in the President of the United States. While you are probably innocent, you were in the White House when all this took place."

"But who will replace me?"

The door opened and in walked the New New Nixon. "I'm sorry about this, Dick," the New New Nixon said, "but the country comes first."

The New New Nixon sat down in the President's chair and started dictating the speech he gave that Monday night.

As the New Nixon left the room, the New New Nixon told a friend, "This is the most difficult decision I've ever had to make."

DON'T GIVE UP THE SHIP

The Naval Court of Inquiry into the sinking of the SS *Watergate* was held in executive session here last week.

On the stand was Captain Richard M. Nixon, who commanded the ship at the time it went down.

Here is a partial transcript of the hearings which do not violate national security.

"Captain Nixon, the SS *Watergate* sprang a leak on the morning of June 17, 1972. What did you do about it at the time?"

"I didn't think much of it. I was told by my executive officer that seven men had been fooling around in the shower room and the nozzle broke off."

"Did you order an investigation of the incident?"

"Yes, I did, and it was the most thorough investigation ever held on the high seas. I told my officers I wanted to know if anyone on my staff had anything to do with the leak. They reported back to me categorically that no one in the crew except for the seven men was involved in the incident. I accepted this as fact."

"Did you try to repair the damage at the time?"

"There was nothing to repair as far as I was concerned. The seven men were court-martialed, and that was the end of it."

"But isn't it true that during the court-martial of the seven, there were hints that other people were involved in the leak?"

"It was only hearsay. A captain has many enemies on a ship, and I was not about to put credence in a lot of gossip and rumor."

"Now, Captain Nixon, since the leak was not repaired, the lower compartments of the ship began to flood. Didn't you feel at that time you should take some action?"

"I sent my people down to inspect the damage, and they said the ship was completely dry belowdecks."

"You didn't go down to inspect the damage yourself?"

"I had to stay on the bridge. It is a mistake for a captain to know too much about what is going on in the crew's quarters. Besides, I had great faith in my officers and their ability to judge whether the ship was in jeopardy or not."

"Is it true that your communications officer, Lieutenant Ronald Ziegler, kept announcing over the loudspeaker that there was nothing wrong with the ship?"

"Yes, he did it on my orders."

"Then Lieutenant Ziegler hadn't gone below to inspect the damage either?"

"Not to my knowledge. We were getting continual reports

from our legal officer, Lieutenant John Dean III, and he assured us that we were safe and our crew was clean."

"But didn't you get suspicious when the water rose to the main deck?"

"I didn't like it, but I didn't consider it my problem. I've been in storms before, six to be exact, and I've always been able to weather them. Besides, my staff told me not to pay any attention because the ship was built to withstand any kind of pressure."

"When did you decide that you were really in danger?"

"On March 21, 1973, I received some startling information from my officers that the leak did not come from a shower, but that we had really hit an iceberg."

"Then you decided to take action?"

"Yes, I went on the loudspeaker myself and said that anyone responsible for hitting the iceberg would be immediately removed from the crew."

"And when did you decide to abandon ship?"

"When the water got up to my hips and I noticed all my officers starting to take to the lifeboats."

"How did you feel about losing so many of your crew?"

"I felt bad about it, but by that time it was every man for himself."

LEAKING TO THE PRESS

The reason why the Watergate case has broken open is that everyone involved is leaking to the press to save his own skin.

I work in a building on Pennsylvania Avenue which also includes the offices of the Boston *Globe*, *Newsweek* magazine, Newhouse Newspapers, the Dallas *Times-Herald*, the Kansas City *Star*, and the Chicago *Tribune*.

The other morning when I arrived, there was a long line outside the building composed of people implicated in the Watergate affair. The line ran around the block.

A policeman stopped me at the door and said, "Get in the back of the line, Mac, like everybody else. Some of these people have been waiting all night to tell their stories to the press."

"I'm not a suspect in the Watergate case, Officer, I'm a newspaperman going up to my office."

Some people in the line heard me and tried to shove documents at me.

"Let's have none of that," the cop said to the crowd. "You can show him your documents when you get inside."

One man, a former White House aide, shouted, "I can tell you the whole story on the Ellsberg break-in."

Another man said, "He doesn't know anything. I've got Ellsberg's psychiatrist's couch hidden in my home."

Someone down the line said, "Don't listen to him. I have a blockbuster of a story. Howard Hunt and G. Gordon Liddy wrote Clifford Irving's book about Howard Hughes."

Someone else yelled, "I have the names of everyone who contributed a million dollars to the Committee to Reelect the President. Give me a break. I've been waiting since six o'clock last night to leak it."

"I'm sorry," I said to the man, "but I don't write that kind of story. Why don't you leak it to Jack Anderson?"

"You can't get near his office," the man said. "I waited two days to leak it to him, and I never got closer than a block away."

The police officer said to me, "I wish you wouldn't stand out here, sir. These people are desperate, and I don't want a riot."

A man slipped me $5,000 in new $100 bills. "Take me upstairs with you to *Newsweek*'s office, and I'll give you another five thousand."

The offer was tempting, but I gave the man his money back. I said, "It would be unfair to the other suspects in line. I'm sure you'll all get in to leak your stories."

"That's what they told me at the Washington *Post*. But when I got up to the head of the line, they said they didn't need any more on the Watergate bugging. They had enough leaks on *that*."

"I can't understand why all you people are so desperate to talk to the press," I said to several of the people, all former White House aides.

"You dummy," one of them shouted. "If we implicate others, then we can get immunity from prosecution."

"Why should we be the scapegoats?" another man shouted. "We want to get the guys who put us up to this."

"If we get our stories in print," a third said, "then the public will know we were just little fish in a big stagnant pool."

The police officer said, "You can't stay out here, sir. Either go upstairs or to the Sans Souci."

"I'll go upstairs," I said.

The policeman opened the glass door, and the crowd pushed forward waving their incriminating evidence.

He shouted, "All right, you people stop shoving, or I'll make you go to the back of the line."

THE POOR AMERICAN TOURIST—LONDON, ENGLAND

Probably no one has suffered more from the Watergate scandal than the American tourist.

Every time a new revelation comes out the dollar is attacked by money speculators in Europe, and by the end of the day it's worth less than it was in the morning.

The other day I was standing in a London bank trying to cash a $50 traveler's check. In front of me was an Arab sheikh with a porter's trolley on which were ten large bales of American dollars valued at $10,000,000.

"It looks like you're going to have a pretty wild weekend," I said, trying to strike up a conversation.

"Oh, no," he said. "This is just some petty cash I found around the house, and I was afraid of being stuck with it. Tell me, do you think this Watergate business is serious?"

"One never knows," I said guardedly. "Why do you ask?"

"I have thirty million dollars in the Rolls outside, and I didn't know if this would be the best time to sell them. Actually I hadn't intended to come to the bank today, but then I read in the newspapers that John Mitchell said he wouldn't be the fall guy in the Watergate. I decided that if he refused to be the fall guy, then President Nixon would have to be the fall guy, and if that happened, heaven knows what will happen to the American dollar."

"I'm sure President Nixon had nothing to do with the scandal," I said, trying to protect my $50 traveler's check.

"I'm not so sure," the sheikh replied. "I've been watching the hearings on the BBC, and I've been very impressed with McCord's testimony. One of my wives said to me last night, 'Abdul, I think you should get out of dollars and into something more comfortable.' "

"That's silly," I said. "The Watergage will blow over, and then you'll be sorry you sold all those dollars."

"I thought that way myself until I read the John Dean III interview in *Newsweek*. If he can substantiate his charges, the dollar could go right through the floor. I have one hundred million of them in my garage, and I would hate to be saddled with them just before I go on summer vacation."

"Sir," I said, holding on tightly to my traveler's check, "I live in Washington, and I can assure you that the dollar has never been stronger. If I had the gold, I would buy your dollars from you right now."

"Perhaps," said the sheikh, "but I have a rich friend, the Sheikh of Quait, and he advised me to get rid of all my American money while I could. We small sheikhs can't gamble with the few dollars we have."

The man behind us, who turned out to be the treasurer of a large multinational company, asked, "Would you mind moving up? I have to buy twenty million British pounds by noon or my president will have my head."

"Are you buying them with dollars?" I asked.

"I'm not buying them with rubles," he said rather huffily.

The man behind him, who was three feet tall, said in a Swiss accent, "Vat's mit the walk? Move along."

"Who's he?" I asked the treasurer.

"He's a gnome from Switzerland. Every time there's a new development in the Watergate he flies over here to buy German marks. With dollars."

"Why doesn't he buy them in Switzerland?" I asked.

"He's afraid if he does, the Swiss will find out the dollar is in trouble."

"Will you hold my place in the line?" the Arab sheikh asked. "I think I'll go out to the car and get the other thirty million."

"Certainly," I said, "but I have a favor to ask of you in return. I'm an American tourist and I was wondering if I could buy pounds with my fifty-dollar traveler's check before you cash in your dollars. I'm afraid if you cash in first, I might not be able to pay for my hotel room tonight."

The sheikh said, "Are you crazy? What happens if they devalue the dollar before I get to the cashier's window?"

"Nixon wouldn't do that," I said.

"Aha, but what about President Agnew?"

A LONELY JOB

I was walking by the White House the other night when I heard an anguished cry from inside. "Alger Hiss. Where were you when I needed you?"

I thought nothing of it and walked a few more steps. Then I heard the same voice again. "Where were those college bums when I needed them?"

A guard standing by the gate asked, "Can I help you, sir?"

"That voice coming from inside. It's so eerie."

"Aye," he said, "it's been going on for weeks now. It does give you the willies."

"Who's in there?" I asked.

"Nobody. The house is empty."

"Empty?"

"Aye, they all moved out. There's nobody there."

"But the voice. I heard a voice."

"That you did. They say the place is haunted, and full of ghosts."

I heard the voice again. "Ehrlichman, Haldeman, Kleindienst, Gesundheit."

"Do you believe in ghosts?" I asked the man.

"After what's been happening around here for the last two months, I don't know what to believe any more. I reported the voice to my superiors, and they told me to forget it. They said if anyone asked me, I heard nothing."

"You mean it's another cover-up?" I asked.

"I just follow orders. They say it's a matter of executive privilege, and I can't talk about anything I've heard here, even if it's a ghost who has done the talking."

"It must be lonely work."

"Aye, that it is. Sometimes when the fog rolls in the Rose Garden, I think I hear the U.S. Marine Band playing 'Hail to the Chief.' Once, I saw the White House guards marching in their old uniforms."

The voice came out loud and clear again. "Martha, Martha, why have you deserted me?"

"The voice sounds so familiar," I told the guard.

"That it does. It's somebody I know, but I can't make out who."

"I'm sure it isn't Lincoln."

"And it isn't FDR," the guard said.

"Lyndon Baines Johnson had more of a twang in his voice."

The guard scratched his head. "It beats me."

"When did they board up the house?"

"About three weeks ago. It seems after all the trouble, they couldn't get anyone to work here. The secretaries were frightened, and after the big shots left, no one would take their place. So they closed it down and moved to Camp David."

The voice again: "In our own lives let each of us ask—not just what government will do for me, but what can I do for myself?"

"You don't have any grass on you?" the guard asked.

"No, I'm sorry I don't. Why do you ask?"

"I don't know. You hang around here for a little while, and pot kind of makes you forget what's going on. Tell you the truth, mister, I really got the shakes."

"Why don't you go to a psychiatrist?"

"Not on your life. If I did, somebody would break in his office and steal my records."

THE NEVER-ENDING WATERGATE SAGA

It was May, 1975, and the Watergate hearings were still being televised every day. It was the longest show in the history of television, and like *The Forsyte Saga*, it was hard to keep all the characters straight.

The Bilkin family sat in front of their set bleary-eyed, but determined to see it through.

On the stand was John Dean III, who had been testifying every day for eight months.

Maude Bilkin said, "What a nice-looking boy. Tricia made a smart choice marrying him."

"Tricia isn't married to John Dean," Alan Bilkin said. "She's married to Jeb Magruder."

The Bilkins' sixteen-year-old daughter, Ellie, spoke up. "I thought Julie was married to Jeb Magruder and Tricia was married to Senator Sam Ervin."

"No," said Joel, the eighteen-year-old son. "Sam Ervin is married to Martha Mitchell. Their son is Henry Kissinger."

Maude replied, "I thought Henry Kissinger was the nephew of John Ehrlichman."

Alan Bilkin shook his head. "No, don't you remember last year it was revealed that Henry Kissinger was H. R. Haldeman's long-lost son?"

"That's right," Joel said. "And Henry Kissinger and Martha Mitchell were in love but they broke up when G. Gordon Liddy tapped their telephone."

"Didn't Martha Mitchell marry Maurice Stans?" Ellie asked.

"No, she married Robert Vesco and moved to Costa Rica," Maude said.

"I don't remember that," Alan said.

"You were working that day," Maude explained.

"What happened to Dick Helms?" Alan asked.

"Dick Helms became the head of the Bureau of Indian Affairs and lost a finger at Wounded Knee," Joel said.

"I thought Bebe Rebozo was at Wounded Knee," Ellie said.

"No, Bebe Rebozo became the governor of Florida when Daniel Ellsberg was appointed the head of the CIA," Alan said.

"Wasn't Daniel Ellsberg Patrick Gray's lawyer?" Maude asked.

"No, Ron Ziegler was Patrick Gray's lawyer. But then he

resigned to become the commandant of the U.S. Marine Corps," Joel said.

"I thought Richard Kleindienst was made the commandant," Ellie said.

"No, Kleindienst became the head of ITT after Dita Beard moved to Denver," Alan said.

"It does seem hard to follow," Maude said. "Let's listen."

Ellie said, "Dean seems to be talking about President Nixon."

"What happened to President Nixon?" Joel asked.

"He married Brezhnev's daughter," Alan said.

Maude replied, "It seems to me Spiro Agnew's son married Brezhnev's daughter. I think Nixon is still married to Pat."

"But if Nixon is still married to Pat, what happened to Donald Segretti?" Ellie asked.

"He was adopted by Senator and Mrs. Muskie and now lives in Maine with Jane Fonda," Alan said.

"I thought Jane Fonda had fallen in love with Daniel Ellsberg's psychiatrist," Joel said.

"I don't remember that," Maude said.

"You were shopping that day," Joel replied.

"Do you think John Dean will go to jail?" Ellie asked.

"I hope not," said Maude. "It would be awfully tough on Tricia."

WATERGATE DAY

On June 17 the United States celebrated the first anniversary of the breaking in of the Watergate. A group of patriotic citizens under the leadership of a friend of mine, Julian Stein, urged President Nixon to declare it a national holiday.

He told me, "The one thing England has that we don't is Guy Fawkes Day. For over three hundred and sixty-five years the British have indulged in all sorts of shenanigans in memory of the man who tried to blow up Parliament in the Gunpowder Plot of 1605. Among other things they burn Guy Fawkes in effigy, make huge bonfires, and set off firecrackers. In further commemoration of the plot, a formal and ritualistic search of the vaults beneath the Houses of Parliament is made each year at the opening of their sessions.

"We think that June 17 should be duly celebrated in the country as Watergate Day."

"It sounds great," I said. "What would people do to observe it?"

On Watergate Day Americans would memorialize this historic event by taping other people's doors, tapping telephones, spying on their neighbors, using aliases, wearing red wigs, and making inoperative statements."

"You mean people could lie to each other?" I asked.

"Of course. Parents would not have to tell the truth to their children, bosses would not have to level with their employees, and husbands would be permitted to make up stories to tell their wives."

"June 17 would be like April Fool's Day," I said.

"It would be much wilder. Anyone breaking into a doctor's office would be granted immunity. People could raise money for phony causes, and only cash would be accepted as legal tender."

"Would you have parades?" I asked Mr. Stein.

"You bet you would. You would have plumbers' parades all over the country, honoring the plumbers in the White House who were supposed to turn off all the leaks.

"In Washington the President would review the CIA and FBI bands as they marched down Pennsylvania Avenue leading the loyal members of the Committee to Reelect the President.

"In the afternoon the President would lay a wreath at the Watergate complex just under the window of the former Headquarters of the Democratic National Party."

"That would be nice," I said.

"In the evening there would be a fireworks display in every town to remind us all of the fireworks the Watergate has caused in this country."

"I get chills just thinking about it," I admitted.

"If the President declares June 17 a national holiday, you could have Watergate Day Sales in the department stores with giant savings on burglar tools, shredding machines, and lie detectors. And grand juries would only have to work half a day.

"Of course," added Mr. Stein, "the churches would remain open for people who wanted to pray for their country."

"I don't see anything wrong with it," I said. "There's only one question. In England on Guy Fawkes Day they burn Guy Fawkes in effigy. Who would Americans burn in effigy on Watergate Day?"

"We may have to wait until June 17, 1974, before we figure that one out."

II. WHERE IS THE PRESIDENT?

FUTURE SHOCK

We are all going through a period of adjustment in our thinking in this country. The things we grew up believing in do not necessarily hold true anymore, and the sooner we face up to reality, the healthier this nation will be. Here are some of the truisms that no longer are valid.

Congress is an equal branch of government.

All the Europeans want from us is our American dollars.

Teach a man a trade and he can get a job.

If you live in the country, you don't have to lock your doors.

A woman's place is in the home.

What every town needs is lots of industry.

The best school is the one nearest you.

Everyone in the United States has to pay taxes.

An American President *cannot* get us into a war without the approval of Congress.

If you treat children like grown-ups, they'll behave like grown-ups.

Most doctors make house calls.
You can have a happy marriage if you take Geritol.
Only perverts go to X-rated movies.
You can have a good day if you eat a healthy breakfast.
If you go to college, you'll make something of yourself.
Your children will support you in your old age.
Social Security is enough to live on when you reach sixty-five.
All policemen are honest.
Black people prefer to live among their own.
Baseball is the national sport.
Oil is the best form of heating.
You *can't* live in a world where half the people are enslaved.
The First Amendment protects the press.
The way to a man's heart is through his stomach.
The best things in life are free.
The law of the land is the law of the land.
The public has a right to know.
If you go outside, you'll get a breath of fresh air.
The Attorney General of the United States represents all the people.
America has the best postal service in the world.
Teachers never strike.
If you work hard, your fellow union workers will admire you.
The American people will receive a peace dividend after the Indochinese war is ended.
What's good for General Motors is good for the country.
Women who enjoy sex are sick.
If you save the Defense Department money, you are automatically promoted.
The United States plans to ration gasoline only in time of war.
The President lives in the White House.

THE NEW ENEMY

Every country needs an enemy to call its own. You really can't have a foreign policy or a giant defense establishment unless your national security is threatened by another nation.

President Nixon has been moving so fast to mend fences with our former enemies that there is some question in the post-Vietnamese war era as to which country will play the role of the heavy in U.S. foreign affairs.

A team of top diplomats and military men has been working on the problem for more than a year under the direction of Heinrich Himmelfarb, a deputy to Henry Kissinger.

Himmelfarb, who is known in the White House as the "Kraut's Kraut," told me, "It isn't easy to find an enemy since the President visited Peking. Once Pat Nixon was shown on television eating won ton soup with Chou En-lai, we had to eliminate China as the number one threat to America."

"What about Russia?" I asked.

"They're buying all our wheat. You can't make an enemy out of a country that's helping your balance of payments."

"Cuba?" I suggested.

"We've considered Cuba, but since we're trying to work out an antihijacking treaty, the President thinks it best to cool it as far as Cuba is concerned."

"But we have to have an enemy," I said. "Every nation needs another country it can hate."

"We're aware of that," Himmelfarb replied. "And we think we have one."

"You have?"

Himmelfarb went over to a large globe in his office and stuck his finger menacingly near the top of it. "It's Sweden."

"Sweden?"

"Yes," said Himmelfarb, his eyes burning. "Sweden is a threat to the security of the United States and the free world. Unless our country arms itself and takes a stand, half the world will become Swedish."

"It's that serious?" I asked.

"Ideologically, Sweden is against everything we believe in. They're for free medical care, free help for the poor, free homes for the aged, and free love for everyone. The United States cannot sit by and allow them to spread their message to the rest of the globe."

"Blimey," I said.

"The FBI has uncontrovertible evidence that Sweden has

financed Swedish massage parlors all over the United States. These parlors are being used to lull American men into a false sense of security. Swedish films have been used to subvert the young and the disenfranchised. We know for a fact that the Sexual Revolution is being plotted and administered directly from Stockholm."

"Who would have thought it?"

"Swedish tankers have been following the Sixth Fleet; Swedish freighters have been seen in New York Harbor; Swedish airplanes have flown over Los Angeles. The American people must be alerted to these acts of aggression, which we cannot take lying down."

"But it's so hard to hate a Swede," I said.

"Why is it hard? They took in our American deserters and draft dodgers. They organized demonstrations against the Vietnamese conflict. And they did the unforgivable when they criticized President Nixon's Christmas bombing of Hanoi. If that isn't an enemy of the United States, then I don't know what the word means."

"But surely if President Nixon has made his peace with China and the Soviet Union, he can find some way of resuming diplomatic relations with Sweden."

"Not as long as Sweden continues to enslave its people and spread its diabolical massage parlors around the world."

NO PEACE DIVIDEND

The day after President Nixon gave his report to Congress on his trip to the Soviet Union, I went over to see my friend Hannibal Stone, president of the Association for a Permanent Military-Industrial Complex.

Because the President had announced agreement on the freeze of nuclear weapons with the Soviets, I expected Hannibal to be depressed. Instead, I found him euphoric.

"Hannibal," I said, "how can you be smiling when President Nixon and the Russians are talking about disarmament? Surely this is a blow to the military-industrial complex and all it stands for."

"Wrong," Hannibal said, handing me a cigar. "This is the best thing that could happen to us."

"I don't understand," I said, as he lit my cigar with a Minuteman missile cigarette lighter.

"Russia and the United States have agreed to limit antiballistic missiles. They have also agreed to freeze land-based and submarine-based intercontinental missiles at the level now in operation. If it works, they may come to new agreements to limit arms production on other weapons now being made. This means we will have to work twice as hard to develop new weapons that aren't covered by the arms agreements."

"You mean we're not going to save any money by the signing of the arms treaty?"

"*Au contraire,*" Hannibal said. "We will have to spend more money now for defense than ever before."

"Damn it, Hannibal," I said. "I was hoping for a peace dividend."

"Forget the peace dividend," Hannibal said. "In order for the Joint Chiefs of Staff to assure us that we have adequate protection in spite of the arms accord, we're going to have to spend at least another twenty billion dollars in new weaponry—stuff that hasn't even been dreamed of yet."

"I knew the President's speech was too good to be true."

"You must remember," Hannibal said, "the military-industrial complex makes very little money once it is in full production on a weapon. By then everyone knows exactly what the weapon is going to cost, and we can't monkey around with the figures.

"But when we're asked to develop a new weapon, no one can put a price tag on it, and the longer it doesn't work, the more money we can ask for to develop it.

"Give me a contract for a weapon no one understands, and I'll give you twice the profits that I would on a weapon that has proved itself in the field."

"Gosh darn, Hannibal," I said. "I thought one of the reasons the President went to Moscow was to cut down on the spiraling inflation and wasteful money both countries were spending on weapons."

"Maybe he did," Hannibal said. "But the fact is that at this very moment members of the Soviet military-industrial complex are at their drafting boards working on new weapons which are not part of the accords. We can't let the Russians get ahead of us on these weapons or we will lose the military edge to the other superpower."

"But you don't even know what those weapons are," I protested.

"All the more reason to spend money developing our weapons. I would say that the President's nuclear arms accord is actually a breakthrough for us.

"Now we can come up with any wild idea and Congress will have to buy it. We can say that if we don't have this weapon, the Russians may have one that is much more devastating. The Soviet military-industrial complex is probably going to use the same ploy with their people."

I said, "President Eisenhower warned me about people like you."

Hannibal chuckled and slapped me on the shoulder. "Don't let it get you down. It's only money. Here, take the Minuteman missile cigarette lighter with you. Consider it a peace dividend from me."

THE GODFATHER NEVER FORGIVES

"Godfather, now that the war with the Hanoichese family is over, I have a favor to ask of you."

"What is it, my son?"

"Will you forgive all those involved in the recent unpleasantness?"

"Of course I will. I am sending my *consigliore*, 'Henry the Kiss,' to see the Hanoichese family this week and make them an offer they can't refuse."

"I wasn't thinking about the Hanoichese, Godfather. I was thinking about members of your *own* family."

"You want me to forgive members of my own family?"

"The war is finished, Godfather. Why do you still hold a grudge against the people you live with?"

THE GODFATHER NEVER FORGIVES

"Because they did not support me when I was fighting the Hanoichese. Everyone makes mistakes, but we all have to pay for our mistakes."

"We have to heal the wounds of the family, Godfather. We have to rebuild the morale of the organization which was ruined by the war. The family is in shambles."

"Well, let me tell you something. I could have worked out a deal with the Hanoichese family long ago had it not been for members of my own family who kept encouraging the Hanoichese family to continue the fighting. I wanted a peace with honor. But all they were screaming was 'Stop the bombing.' They wanted me to cut and run. But I wouldn't listen to them. And now they're going to suffer. I am going to make them pay for their disloyalty."

"Godfather, what good is it to have the family at one another's throats? If you can live with the Hanoichese and Kremlinchio and Pekinatti families, surely you can find a way to live with your own family."

"The first thing the Godfather must have from his people is loyalty. I will not make peace with this sellout brigade. I know they hate me. They've always hated me. But I don't care if they hate me or not. Do you want to know why?"

"Why, Godfather?"

"Because I hate them. A Godfather must be tough, ruthless. Forgiveness is a sign of weakness. It's no problem to forgive my enemies, but I can never pardon members of my own family for criticizing the way I ran the war."

"I agree it's hard to forgive. But what you need now is the respect and allegiance of everyone in the family. You can't get that by continuing to hate the ones who disagreed with you."

"You don't know me very well. I don't want respect and allegiance. I want them to hurt; all of them—particularly the ones who called me names behind my back. I want them to crawl on their knees to me and kiss my feet."

"Then will you forgive them?"

"No."

"Well, at least it's good to know where you stand."

"My son, after we made a deal with the Hanoichese, I could have done the popular thing, the easy thing, and made peace with my own family. But I chose the unpopular way, the hard way. I chose to shaft the rats in my own family who made my life so miserable for the last four years."

"All right, Godfather. What are your orders?"

"I want to put out a contract on George McGovern, Frank Church, Ramsey Clark, Jane Fonda, Dr. Spock, Bishop Paul Moore, Teddy Kennedy, and William Fulbright, for starters. We'll take care of the newspapers later. We're going to clean out this family once and for all."

STATE'S COVER IS BLOWN

One of the best-kept secrets of the Nixon administration was blown during the President's trip to China. The American people discovered that there is a highly confidential organization advising the President on foreign affairs which is called the State Department. The head of this secret *apparat* is a lawyer named William Rogers, an old friend of President Nixon.

This is how the existence of this undercover agency was revealed. When President Nixon went to China, he was seen in the company of a sandy-haired man who rarely left the President's side. Most reporters on the trip assumed he was a Secret Service man and paid no attention to him.

But then the President went to visit Chairman Mao Tse-tung, and the newspapermen discovered that the sandy-haired man did not accompany Mr. Nixon. This knocked out the theory that the mysterious person was a Secret Service agent.

When questioned about what the person was doing on the trip, Ron Ziegler reluctantly admitted that the man's name was William Rogers and he held the title of Secretary of State, and he had something to do with foreign affairs, though Ziegler refused to go into it any further.

Meanwhile, back in Washington, reporters were trying to find out more about the State Department and where it fitted into the diplomatic picture.

The White House seemed very disturbed about the leak, and J. Edgar Hoover was ordered to find out who blew Mr. Rogers' cover.

A White House spokesman told me, "It does no good for the security of the nation to talk about the role of the State Department in foreign affairs. The people who revealed the existence of Mr. Rogers and the agency he represents may believe they were reporting news, but in effect they are only giving aid and comfort to the enemy."

"Does the revelation of a State Department mean that Henry Kissinger is not running the entire foreign policy of the United States?"

"It means no such thing. All policies on foreign affairs are still made by the 'Department of Kissinger' or, as we call it here, the DOK. The State Department—and I'm not confirming there is one, mind you—is sort of a backup organization which provides the President with information he might miss from his usual sources."

"If this is true, why all the mystery about the organization? Why hasn't the country heard about the State Department before? And why has the identity of William Rogers, as head of it, been kept a secret?"

"The President believes that there are certain agencies that can operate better if they are not publicized. If people knew what Mr. Rogers did, he would not have the freedom of movement that he has now. He can go anywhere in the world without being recognized. The President can assign him missions that would be impossible for someone as well known as Henry Kissinger to take. The State Department, because of its anonymity, has been able to perform a great service to the nation."

"Do you believe the gamble of taking Mr. Rogers to Peking was worth all the trouble that the State Department is now in?"

"That's Monday morning quarterbacking. From the beginning we were aware that it was a calculated risk to allow Mr. Rogers to be seen in such close proximity to the President. But at the time the decision was made, we had no idea that the President would meet Mao Tse-tung, and Rogers wouldn't."

"Will the State Department be dismantled, now that its role is out in the open?"

"That decision is up to Dr. Kissinger."

THE PRESIDENT'S PURGE

It was a grim week in the White House. After his landslide
election, instead of getting even with the Democrats, President
Nixon surprised everyone by announcing that he was purging
the Republicans who helped him get elected. Everyone with a
high administration job was asked to hand in his resignation.

One source in the White House told me exactly what kind of
week it was:

Pat Nixon came into the President's office.

"Look what someone just gave me," she said angrily.

"What is it, Pat?" the President asked.

"It's a resignation form to fill out. Are you asking me to
resign?"

"It's just a formality," President Nixon said. "I've asked
everyone in the White House to resign so I can get rid of the
people I don't want."

"But that's unfair," Pat protested. "I worked very hard for
you during the campaign."

"Of course you did, Pat, and I told Haldeman and Ehrlichman to take that into consideration. I said, 'When we go over
the list of the people we're dropping, keep in mind that Pat was
at my side during the three times I left the White House to
campaign.' "

Mrs. Nixon held the resignation in her hand and said
tearfully, "You would think after all these years there would be
no question about my staying with you for your second term."

"Now don't get upset, Pat," the President said. "I owe you a
lot, but I have to do what's best for America. I can't give special
favors to any group, nor can I as President favor one person in
the White House family over another. I assure you we will take
a close look at your record before we make any definite
decision."

"Dick, don't you remember the Checkers speech, the stoning
in South America, your defeats in 1960 and 1962? I was the
only one who didn't turn her back on you. Doesn't that count
for something?"

"It does, Pat. We've not only got all those facts, but we have your FBI record as well. On the basis of all this I would guess you have a better than fifty-fifty chance of staying in the White House. But it isn't my decision alone. The purge staff has to look at the big picture. How much money is it costing us? Is the person doing more than his share of the work he is assigned? Was he involved in the Watergate bugging affair? And finally, is the job worth not eliminating altogether?"

"I went with you to China, I went with you to Russia, I went with you to Iran. Surely that must mean a lot to you."

"It does, Pat. The boys were very impressed with those trips, and it's a big plus. At the same time, the next four years are going to be the most important in the history of the United States. I can't afford to make any mistakes if I want my rightful place in history. That is why I asked for everyone's resignation. There is too much deadwood in my administration."

"Suppose I refuse to resign?"

"Pat, please don't put me in that position. You've meant a lot to me during all these years, and I would hate our relationship to end on a bitter note. I assure you that when your name comes up in the meeting, I'll be fighting for you to stay on, even if we have to change your job designation."

"Thank you, Dick," Pat said. "I appreciate that."

Just then the door flew open, and Julie Nixon Eisenhower and Tricia Nixon Cox burst in.

"Daddy," cried Tricia, "they've asked us to resign!"

"Good grief," the President said exasperatedly. "I can't save *everybody*."

THE DIRTY TRICKS DEPARTMENT

It took the President's White House staff all day to locate the Old Nixon. They finally found him at Howard Johnson's across the street from the Watergate, eating a meat loaf sandwich.

"You'd better get back to the White House right away," John Ehrlichman told him. "The boss is really steaming."

When the Old Nixon walked into the President's office, he found the New Nixon in a rage.

"I've just received information that you're behind the Dirty Tricks Department of the Committee for the Reelection of the President. What do you have to say for yourself?"

"I refuse to comment as I don't want to prejudice the rights of the defendants in the Watergate bugging trial."

"Don't hand me that stuff," the President said. "You've put me in a helluva spot! How could you do it to me?"

"Ah, come on. You're overreacting. We were just having a little fun with the Democrats. No one takes it seriously," the Old Nixon said.

"But we didn't need it," the New Nixon said. "We're ahead by twenty-eight percent in the polls. It makes us look cheap and unscrupulous."

The Old Nixon retorted, "Sure, you can say that now. But at the time we started the intelligence operation, no one knew what was going to happen. Suppose it had been real close? Our Dirty Tricks Department could have made the difference. You've been President so long you don't even understand politics anymore."

"And you've been out of it so long," the New Nixon said, "you don't understand I am more interested in my place in history than I am in some rotten espionage operation against the other political party. I'm being clobbered in the press by all this publicity."

"Will you stop worrying about your place in history? We took a survey, and it showed that the public couldn't care less about the Watergate and the other things that have come out concerning our operation. The attitude is 'Everyone does it during an election year.' "

"That's just swell," the New Nixon said sarcastically. "But do you know how many man-hours the Justice Department, the FBI, and the White House have spent on this problem? I've had to promise a complete and open investigation of every facet of the case."

"And you've done a good job on it, Dickey boy," the Old Nixon chortled. "They won't be able to lay a finger on us before election day."

"Don't be so smug," the New Nixon said. "You've made a mess of things, and I'm giving you an order to stay out of the offices of the Committee for the Reelection of the President. I don't want anyone in the White House to have anything to do with my campaign."

"You can't do that to me," the Old Nixon protested. "The Dirty Tricks Department was my baby. It was the only fun I've had in four years. What am I going to do now?"

"You're to stay in your room until election day," the New Nixon said firmly.

"Suppose I don't? Suppose I spill everything to the Washington *Post*?" the Old Nixon asked.

"Don't threaten me, Tricky," the New Nixon said. "If you do anything to further embarrass me or endanger my reelection, I will turn over to Richard Kleindienst everything I know about your involvement with the Howard Hughes loan. Do I make myself perfectly clear?"

The Old Nixon, looking downcast and defeated, said, "Yes, sir, Mr. President."

WHERE IS THE PRESIDENT?

One morning a White House aide walked into President Nixon's office, which is located on a mountain overlooking Camp David, and asked, "Where is the President?"

The man sitting behind the desk said, "I'm the President."

The aide looked at him closely. "No, you're not. You're the Old Nixon. Where's the New Nixon?"

"He's gone. He asked me to take over for him. I want four hundred more raids on North Vietnam, cut the Health, Education and Welfare budget, scrap all public housing, and let's not give any more aid to the farmers."

"Just a minute. What proof do you have that the President gave you his job?"

"Don't push me, boy," the Old Nixon said angrily, "or I'll have you arrested for treason."

The aide rushed out and brought in the chief of the Secret Service. The aide said, "He's done something with the President of the United States!"

The chief yelled to two of his agents, "Don't let anyone leave the compound!" Then he turned to the Old Nixon. "Okay, wise guy, what did you do with the President?"

"I *am* the President," the Old Nixon said. "I have the Presidential seal to prove it."

"We know the President," the chief said. "He's a statesman, a leader, a peacemaker, a friend of all the people. You certainly don't fit that description."

"I keep telling you the President went fishing after the election and he told me to take over. Now you're wasting my valuable time. I have some scores to settle with the press and television people."

"Not so fast, mister," the chief of the Secret Service said. "Something is rotten in Denmark."

The butler came in the room. "When was the last time you saw the President?" the chief asked him.

"I believe it was just before the bombing of Hanoi and Haiphong. He was in his room, and he seemed rather depressed."

"Was anyone with him?"

"I believe Dr. Kissinger and that gentleman sitting in the President's chair there."

"Get Kissinger in here," the chief said.

Two agents brought Kissinger into the office.

"All right, Doctor," the chief said, "where's the President?"

"I don't know," Kissinger said. "I was going to ask you. I'm rather worried about him."

"What happened in the bedroom the last night you were there?"

"Well, there was three of us, the President, the Old Nixon, and myself. I was explaining to the President that the Paris talks were stalemated and peace *was not* at hand. The Old Nixon became furious and shouted he had no intention of the United States becoming the laughingstock of the world. He said we have to bomb the North Vietnamese back into the Stone Age."

"And what did the President say?"

"He didn't say anything. He just went over to the television set and started watching a football game."

"Then what happened?"

"The Old Nixon said to me, 'What are you standing there for? Start the bombing!'

"I looked at the President for confirmation, but all he said was, 'I like the way Larry Brown goes off tackle.' "

"And that's the last time you saw the President?" the chief asked.

"Yes," Kissinger replied. "I didn't hear from him after the bombing so I assumed he was still watching the football game."

The chief of the Secret Service said, "All right. I want a thorough search of all the rooms as well as the grounds. We've got to find the President before January twentieth or else. . . ."

"Or else what?" the butler asked.

The aide replied, pointing at the Old Nixon, "We'll have to swear *him* in as President."

"Oh, my God," said another aide. "Who's going to tell Pat?"

CALLING BOBBY FISCHER

Not long ago President Nixon had to make one of the most important decisions of his administration. He had to decide whether or not he would put a telephone call through to Iceland if Bobby Fischer won the World Championship Chess Tournament.

There hasn't been an antihero like Bobby Fischer in years. His behavior before and during the tournament caused one Washington *Post* reader to write, "Fischer is the only American who can make everyone in the United States root for the Russians."

Based on what Fischer was doing in Iceland, the President's call could have gone something like this:

"Hello, Bobby, this is President Nixon. I just wanted to call and congratulate you on your victory in Iceland."

"Make it short, will you? I'm tired."

"This is a great day for America, Bobby."

"It's a greater day for me. I won a hundred and fifty thousand dollars, and I showed these Icelandic creeps a thing or two."

"You know, Bobby, I almost made the chess team at Whittier College."

"Big deal."

"But I went out for football instead."

"Is that what this call is all about?"

"Now wait a minute, Bobby. I always call anyone who wins a championship for America. I would like to give you a white-tie dinner at the White House when you come back."

"How much will you pay me to come?"

"Pay you? I don't pay people to have dinner at the White House."

"Then what's in it for me?"

"I'll invite the Cabinet, the Supreme Court, the leaders of Congress, and every rich Republican chess player in the country. I'll get Guy Lombardo to play after dinner. It's the least I can do for someone who beat the great Spassky."

"All right. I'll come, but these are my demands: You send the Presidential plane to Iceland to pick me up. You personally meet me at the plane and provide me with a limousine, a suite of rooms, a private tennis court, my own swimming pool, and ten Secret Servicemen so I'm not bugged by the press."

"I think I can do that, Bobby."

"And no television cameras."

"No television cameras?"

"I hate television cameras. They send me into a frenzy. If I see one television camera at the dinner, I'm walking out."

"Don't worry, Bobby. There won't be any television cameras."

"And no talking while I'm eating. I can't eat when people talk."

"It's very difficult to hold a large dinner at the White House and not have anyone talk."

"That's your problem. If I hear noise of any kind, you're going to have to get yourself another world champion chess player."

"Anything you say, Bobby. It's your dinner."

"What time is this shindig of yours going to take place?"

"I thought about eight o'clock."

"I'll be there at nine. I don't like to stand around and make small talk with a lot of stuffed-shirt politicians."

"I understand, Bobby."

"And I'm bringing my own chair. I can't eat when I'm using someone else's chair. And you better know this right now, I don't like bright lights when I'm eating. If the lights are too bright, I don't start the first course."

"No bright lights. I got you, Bobby. I just want to add how proud we all are of you. You're an inspiration to the young people of America."

The President hangs up and calls Richard Helms of the CIA. "Dick, I'm sending the Presidential plane to Iceland to pick up Bobby Fischer. Do me a favor. After he's on board, will you see that it's hijacked to Cuba?"

THE MYSTERY IS SOLVED

The biggest mystery of President Nixon's speech sometime back was when he revealed that Henry Kissinger had made as many as ten secret trips to Paris to negotiate with the North Vietnamese.

Most people who watched the President found it hard to believe that Mr. Kissinger could have gone to Peking twice, Paris 12 times, and Hollywood 456 times.

How, the big question is, can one man do it?

The answer can now be revealed. There is not one Henry Kissinger, but five.

When President Nixon first came into the White House, he knew he was faced with problems all over the world. He also was aware that he needed a foreign affairs expert who could speak in his name. But he didn't want to spread these duties around.

So he contacted the National Institutes of Health in Bethesda, Maryland, and gave them the problem. The NIH said they were working on a project where they could turn out five people completely alike in every respect. All they needed was a model.

The President called in Henry Kissinger, who was then a professor at Harvard, and told him what the President had on his mind. The real Kissinger, who hates to fly, agreed to go along with the plan.

He went out to NIH for a month, and the doctors got to work duplicating exact models of him (most of the volunteers were German scientists who had been laid off by the space program).

Plastic surgeons went to work on the faces. Hair specialists and makeup men were brought in. In a few cases transplants had to be made to get Kissinger's exact measurements.

By trial and error with twelve volunteers, four were finally selected who looked, talked, and appeared to be facsimiles of Kissinger. (The seven volunteers who didn't make it were buried at midnight with full military honors.)

With five Henry Kissingers to work with, President Nixon was able to go ahead with his foreign policy plans.

A special dormitory had been built in the basement of the White House where all the Henry Kissingers lived when they weren't out on a trip.

Whenever the President wanted a Kissinger for an assignment, he spoke into a special microphone attached to a loudspeaker in the dorm: "Who wants to go to Peking?" If more than one Kissinger wanted to go, they would cut cards for it.

If the President needed a Kissinger for a backgrounder in the White House, he would yell down, "Will one of you guys come up to brief the press?"

Or, as in the case of the secret North Vietnamese peace talks, the President would shout, "Send someone up to go to Paris."

One Kissinger would take the duty at Key Biscayne, and another would accompany the President to San Clemente.

The most ingenious part of the strategy was when someone in the White House decided to give Kissinger the image of a swinger. "If we make him a swinger and have him photographed with beautiful women in Hollywood, New York, and Washington, we will have everybody fooled. At the very moment that he's dancing with Jill St. John, one of the other Kissingers will be eating sweet-and-sour pork with Chou En-lai."

While all five Kissingers wanted to play the role of the
swinger, it was decided to give it to the *real* Henry Kissinger, as
a reward for lending his name and his body to the foreign
policy of the United States of America.

"ASK NOT"

I was sitting with Helmut Strudel, president of Strudel Industries, at President Nixon's inauguration. Strudel had donated a
million dollars to the Committee for the Reelection of the
President and had flown all the way into Washington in his
private plane to see what he had gotten for his money.

As the President spoke about international affairs, Strudel
applauded loudly. But when Mr. Nixon started to talk about
domestic matters, my friend became quite upset. The President
said:

"Let each of us remember that America was built not by
government, but by people—not by welfare, but by work—not
by shirking responsibility, but by seeking responsibility."

Strudel began to perspire. "It sounds like he's not going to
bail my company out of bankruptcy," he said worriedly.

"Don't be silly," I told Strudel. "When he speaks of people
on welfare, the President's talking about the little guy who's
freeloading on the government. He is not talking about
companies that get large government subsidies."

The President said, "In the challenges we face together let
each of us ask not just how government can help but how can I
help?"

"You know, of course," Strudel whispered to me, "that my
company has a contract to build four thousand gazebos for the
U.S. Air Force at eight million dollars each. Well, since we got
the order, gazebos have gone up to $10 million, and unless the
government helps us, we won't be able to deliver them."

"Of course the government will help you," I assured Strudel.
"When the President said, 'Ask not what the government will
do for me but what can I do for myself,' he was talking about
teachers and farmers and old people on Social Security, who

are always at the government trough. Contractors are not in that category."

"I hope not," Strudel said, "because I bought a thousand-dollar box at the Inauguration Ball tonight, and I'd hate for it to be empty."

The President seemed to look at us as he said, "I pledge to you that where this government should act, we will act boldly and lead boldly. But just as important is the role that each and every one of us must play as an individual and member of the community."

Strudel said, "They promised me when I made my political contribution that the White House would personally pay for the overruns on my gazebos. But now the President seems to be hedging on it."

"That's just for the public," I assured Strudel. "Everyone knows big business is dependent on Washington, and no administration is going to turn its back on you just because you're losing money on your gazebos."

The President read on, "Let us pledge together to make these next four years the best four years in America's history, so that on its two hundredth birthday, America will be as young and vital as when it began, and as bright a beacon of hope for all the world."

Strudel applauded as the President finished. Then he recognized Klaus Engelfinger of the National Milk Producers League. "What did you think of it?" Strudel asked him.

"I think he could have exempted dairymen when he was talking about people doing more for themselves," Engelfinger said.

"And Grumman Aircraft," the man behind us yelled.

"And Penn Central," a man in a homburg shouted.

"Why leave out Lockheed?" another distinguished guest yelled.

"Or Litton Industries," a guest chimed in.

Strudel seemed to feel better. "See all you guys at the ball."

NOTHING BUT THE TRUTH

There is no doubt in my mind that the Justice Department conducted the most thorough investigation into the Watergate bugging affair that was humanly possible. The fact that they were unable to trace any of the money in the case to any higher-ups in the Committee for the Reelection of the President was good news to all of us who hate to think that any of our political leaders would be involved in such a sordid affair.

Of course there are certain psychological factors at work in such an investigation which no one can control. When the President's own Attorney General is asked to look into a scandal in the President's own party, there is always the suspicion that something was covered up.

The person I feel the most sorry for is the poor bureaucrat in the Justice Department who was called into his superior's office one day and told, "Hapless, the President of the United States of America wants you to investigate the Watergate bugging affair and all its ramifications."

"The President wants me to do that?"

"That is correct, Hapless. He has given specific instructions that he wants to leave no stone unturned in his effort to root out the evildoers who would have the audacity to bug the offices of the Democratic National Committee."

"Gosh, that's a big assignment."

"The President of the United States, who happens to be the President of all the people as well as the leader of the most powerful country in the world, expects you to treat this as just another case."

"He does?"

"That is correct. He has instructed the Attorney General that even if his own political party is involved, and his own close personal friends are to be investigated, and his reelection is at stake, he still wants the truth to be made public at the earliest opportunity."

"Even before November seventh?"

"The President is more concerned in the illegal uses of wiretapping and bugging than he is in what happens on November seventh. You owe it to the President and the Attorney General to see that every bit of evidence in this case is available to the grand jury."

"Why me?"

"Because the President feels that you are the best man for this job. He knows that you will not let personal considerations or your loyal feelings toward him and the great party which he leads interfere with your objective investigation of this dastardly deed.

"He feels, as does the Attorney General, that you will do the job, regardless of jeopardy to your upcoming promotion or the consequences to your future with the Justice Department."

"Is that how they feel? I didn't even know the President knew me."

"He might not know you personally, but he knows that the Attorney General would not assign anyone to this case unless he was certain that this person could not be intimidated by men in high government positions.

"I might add that as your superior I am proud that the Attorney General has selected someone from my staff. I have as much at stake in this thing as you do, Hapless. Whatever you turn up will personally reflect on me as well as this department. We shall all be watching you closely."

"Don't you have a Mafia case I could have instead?"

"No, Hapless. Anyone in this department can investigate a Mafia case. But there are very few men we can trust to handle an investigation this explosive. It is your duty to our President and the Attorney General, whom you will be working for, God willing, for the next four years, to give us the truth and nothing but the truth, so help you God."

III. A SLOW BOAT TO CHINA

THE CHINA EXPERT

When the euphoria was over about our ping-pong match with Red China, people started to think about the significance of a _real_ détente between the United States and the People's Republic of China.

I hadn't given it much thought until I talked to my friend Cutaway at the State Department.

"Well," he said, "it looks like we've made a breakthrough with the People's Republic of China."

"That's good," I said.

"No, that's bad. The Soviets are very mad at us because we're playing table tennis with Chou En-lai."

"That's bad," I said.

"It could be good," Cutaway said. "If the Soviets are afraid of us making a deal with China, they might be more accommodating about the SALT talks on nuclear weapons."

"That's good," I said.

"It could be bad. If the Soviets decide that an America-China pact was a threat to their security, they might insist they need larger nuclear weapons to protect them from the Chinese."

"That's bad."

"It could be good. We might risk the Soviet wrath in order to open up trade with a country of eight hundred million people. The Chinese need everything, and there is no reason why we shouldn't consider them our largest potential customer. It's a very significant market."

"That would be good," I agreed.

Cutaway shook his head. "Bad. In order to sell them stuff, we'd have to buy things from them."

"Is that bad?"

"In a sense it is because the Chinese might undersell the Japanese to get our business. If we bought things cheaper from the Chinese than we did from the Japanese, we could cause an economic disaster in Japan."

"We'd have to put Pearl Harbor on full alert again," I said.

"It would be good, though, if the Japanese realized that they could no longer flood the American market. Then we'd manage to have better trade relations with them."

"That's good."

"Of course, it wouldn't help our employment situation here, because if the Chinese undersold the Japanese—and we can't compete with the Japanese now—there would be less jobs than ever in this country."

"That's bad," I said.

"It's good in this sense: Once we build up a strong trade relationship with China, we could encourage Chinese tourism to this country. You get fifty million Chinese tourists here at one time, and *all* the airlines and hotels would show a profit."

"That would be good."

"The only thing bad about it is that there aren't enough Chinese restaurants to handle them all."

"I was afraid of that," I said. "What else do you see coming out of the détente?"

"The reason Secretary Laird said we had to build an ABM system was to protect us from the Red Chinese. If we eventually become their friends, we won't need the system."

"That's good," I said.

"But it will already have been built by then and cost the country fifty billion dollars."

"That's bad."

"Don't be too sure. If we take up with the Red Chinese, we might need the ABM system to protect us from Chiang Kai-shek's missiles."

"Which we sold him," I pointed out.

Cutaway sighed. "Ping-pong sure screwed up this country's diplomatic game plan."

A SLOW BOAT TO CHINA

One of the greatest penalties the American people will have to pay for any détente with Red China will be sitting through hours of television film and reading hundreds of articles by American correspondents who have been lucky enough to get a Chinese visa.

Since we have had no reporting from China in twenty years, the media is going to make it up to us in one big gulp, and we'd better be prepared for the results.

These are some of the exciting things we can expect to learn about China in the next year—over and over again:

The Chinese people have enough to eat and seem to be well clothed, though there is no variety in their choice of clothes.

The children smile a lot and look very happy in their schools.

Mao Tse-tung's picture can be seen everywhere.

The Great Wall of China is breathtaking and goes on for miles.

The factories are primitive but are producing goods.

The complexion of Chinese girls is healthy, particularly those who work in the fields.

The streets are very clean.

Foreigners are considered a curiosity.

The Chinese have an abiding fear of the Soviet Union.

There are many parks in China where families go to picnic.

There are no rickshaw boys in Shanghai.

Chinese people like to go to the movies.

The Cultural Revolution was responsible for many changes in the country.

You see a lot of soldiers on the streets.

Chinese footwear does not compare to anything in the West but is adequate.

Mao Tse-tung is given credit for the Great Leap Forward.

Chinese government officials are polite but do not open up to Western correspondents.

Ping-pong is the number one sport in China.

Hotels and restaurants in Peking are surprisingly cheap.

You can't take photographs of military installations.

While the Chinese like Americans personally, they fear the imperialism of the United States.

Chinese opera and ballet are filled with anti-Western propaganda.

Chinese trains and planes are very clean.

There are loudspeakers everywhere blaring out the best thoughts of Mao.

Tipping in China is forbidden.

The Chinese are very honest people, and you can put your camera down and come back an hour later and find it.

The Chinese have very poor-quality toilet paper.

The telephone system doesn't work very well.

You don't see many cars on the roads.

The Chinese do a lot of exercise in the morning.

There are no prostitutes in Peking.

The streets are much safer in China than they are in America.

This gives you just some idea of what the American television viewer and newspaper reader will have to put up with as each new correspondent makes his report on the inscrutable and mysterious People's Republic.

I suppose it's a small price to pay for a free press. But I'm warning the media right now, there are just so many pictures of the Great Wall that the American people can take.

DOES ANYONE KNOW "CHOPSTICKS"?

Despite all the excitement about President Nixon's announced visit to China, everyone remained calm in Washington, and there were very few visible signs that people were affected by it.

It's true that White House aides were eating with chopsticks, and large posters of Henry Kissinger appeared all over town with the legend LET A THOUSAND FLOWERS BLOOM and many Republican officials ordered fireworks to celebrate Mao Tse-tung's birthday.

But the mood here was still one of wait-and-see.

There are many problems which must be resolved before any normal relations can take place between these two great powers.

First, there is the question of a name. It's impossible for anyone in this town to keep referring to "the People's Republic of China."

It's too long, and it certainly doesn't fit into a headline. Many people would like to go back to "Commie China." Others would like to refer to it as "Red China," and then there are, of course, the names that Taiwan would like to call it.

So the first order of business for Mr. Nixon is to say to Chou En-lai, "Before we get down to business, could you come up with a new name for your country so it doesn't take so long to say on television?"

There are some people in Washington who are still suspicious that the People's Republic of China will not change its attitude toward the United States because of President Nixon's visit.

But a China watcher I know said that there is no country in the world that can change its mind faster than the People's Republic of China.

"All Mao Tse-tung has to do is announce that he just had a good thought about the United States, and everyone in the country will have the same thought the next day.

"That is the beauty of dealing with a country which has had a Cultural Revolution."

My China watcher friend says his fear is not that the Peoples' Republic of China will reject President Nixon's friendly over-tures, but that they will embrace them and insist on a trade pact with the United States.

"Can you imagine eight hundred million people," he asked, "making shoes for the United States?"

Projecting the consequences of having the People's Republic

of China as a friend rather than an enemy, my friend said,
"Suppose we were obligated to open the United States to
Chinese tourism, and they started sending over group tours of a
million people at a time? They could collapse our transportation system overnight."

As if this wasn't enough to worry about, my friend warned,
"The reason why the People's Republic of China is willing to
start up relations with us is that they have had no experience
with American tourists. Once they open the doors to American
tourists, U.S. relations will be as bad with China as they now
are with France."

But all this is conjecture, and no one knows what will happen
from here on out.

This could be the dawning of a new age in which we would
see Mao Tse-hiltons sprouting up all over China, with Tricia
Nixon and her husband, Eddie Cox, taking each other's picture
at the Great Wall and Martha Mitchell sailing down the
Yangtze with her parasol.

Or it could end in disaster and in five years produce a new
Senator Joe McCarthy, who would say at a televised hearing,
"Now, Mr. Kissinger, will you tell the committee in your own
words exactly what happened when you got an upset stomach
in Pakistan?"

WHAT DID THEY DO TO SCOTTY?

My good friend James "Scotty" Reston of the New York *Times*
had his appendix taken out at the anti-imperialist hospital in
Peking. According to Reston's reports, he received excellent
care from the Chinese doctors, and they treated him like a
king—well, like an anti-imperialist peasant anyway.

But as I read the article about the removal of Scotty's
appendix, a terrible thought crossed my mind. What if the
Chinese, unknown to Reston, put something back in place of
the appendix?

Suppose, and I must admit I have no basis for it except a
wicked imagination, the Chinese sewed a tiny radio transmitter

in Scotty's insides, so that no matter where he went in the world, they could hear everything someone is saying to him.

Everyone knows that Scotty talks to the most important people in the world. The Chinese also would have assumed that as soon as he came back to the United States, he would see President Nixon. What better listening post would the People's Republic of China have in the White House than James Reston's stomach?

Knowing how the Chinese work, all they would have to do is have one of their agents stationed within a mile of Scotty with a receiver and they would be able to record everything that goes on in the highest branches of government.

In fairness to the People's Republic of China, they probably didn't plan to sew a bug in Scotty.

As far as they were concerned, he was just another aggressor and running dog of the Western capitalist lackey press. But when good fortune struck and Scotty's appendix started to ache, the top Chinese Secret Service people must have realized they had a golden opportunity.

The big problem they probably faced was to find a transmitter that could not only take a beating in Scotty's innards, but would also have enough power to survive for any period of time.

Fortunately, the Chinese had the solution. Owing to excellent scientific achievements, the People's Republic anti-imperialist laboratories have perfected a tiny new battery which works on monosodium glutamate. Knowing Reston's penchant for Chinese food, which contains large doses of monosodium glutamate, the powers in Peking have no fear that the transmitter will work for years. One egg roll alone can keep Scotty's bug sending out signals for eighteen months.

While this in itself could make Scotty a walking security risk, some people here in Washington fear that the Chinese may have gone even further and inserted not only a listening transmitter, but the X104 Mao Tse-tung minispeaker. If they did this, a Red Chinese agent, by twisting a dial, could make Scotty spout Mao Tse-tung's thoughts at the most inopportune time.

If, for example, he were asked in front of a Senate committee why the New York *Times* printed the Pentagon Papers, Reston might get up and yell:

"Because all reactionaries are paper tigers, and the feudal landlord class and slaveowning bourgeoisie must be alerted to the people's struggle to overthrow the chains and impotent thinking of the misguided intellectuals and lackey counterrevolutionary followers of our corrupt leaders."

Now this sort of thing could be embarrassing, not only to Reston, but also to the New York *Times*.

I wish to restate that I have no evidence that anything was done to Scotty at the anti-imperialist hospital in Peking other than to remove his appendix. But I don't think we should take any chances. What I'm trying to say to you, Scotty, wherever you are, is that for the nation's security, we're going to have to cut you open again as soon as you come home.

THE RED CHINA LOBBY CROWD

Whether President Nixon planned it or not, his trip to China created an elite White House press corps that split the correspondents in Washington asunder.

By choosing 87 TV commentators, technicians, newspapermen, and columnists out of 2,000 applicants, Mr. Nixon conferred the nearest thing to knighthood on the correspondents making the trip.

The White House press room was divided between those who got their cholera shots and those who didn't.

"The Red China Lobby Crowd," as they were bitterly referred to by the newspapermen who weren't going, were easy to identify because they kept waving the *Little Red Books* of Mao Tse-tung during last week's press briefings.

They also could be found in the Executive Office Building cafeteria eating their chili and beans with chopsticks.

In fairness to the Red China Lobby Crowd, they tried to keep a low profile once the list of those who would accompany President Nixon was posted. Many went out of their way to be nice to those who hadn't been chosen. One of them gave out free fortune cookies during Henry Kissinger's briefings. Another served jasmine tea during a poker game in the lounge. Others handed out bowls of rice to their news-hungry fellow correspondents.

But despite this outward display of friendship, there was a feeling on the part of those who weren't going with President Nixon that the Red China Lobby Crowd was patronizing them.

There was nothing anyone could put his finger on, but there were little things that added up. One correspondent who was making the trip refused to take off his quilted Mao jacket in the press room. Another had his name in Chinese plastered on his portable typewriter, and still another man kept referring to those who weren't going as "counterrevolutionaries."

Adding insult to injury, the 87 elitists did exercises every morning in front of a portrait of Mao on the White House lawn. This was followed by a ten-mile swim down the Potomac, where they shouted slogans of support for the Cultural Revolution.

As if this weren't enough, some of the Red China Lobby Crowd started to confess their sins publicly in front of Ron Ziegler and asked to be sent to state farms after their trip so they could be "rehabilitated."

One White House correspondent who had been turned down said, "I don't give a damn how the elitists behave now. After eight days in China they'll all be experts, and God help us when they start spinning their tales of what happened to them when they visited a tire factory in Peking."

Another disgruntled White House correspondent said, "I can just hear future White House briefings when every question by the elitists will be preceded by 'Ron, when Chou En-lai told us . . .' or 'As you recall, Ron, you denied in Shanghai. . . .' "

It is obvious that the White House press room will never be the same again. By making his trip to China, Mr. Nixon has been able to destroy the morale of the press corps forever. Using divide-and-conquer tactics, he has managed to turn brother correspondent against brother.

The President may not have resolved his diplomatic problems by going to Peking, but he put the men covering him at the

White House in disarray, and that, as Vice President Agnew would agree, is worth all the tea in China.

MAO COMES TO AMERICA

Every one of us who was glued to the TV set when President Nixon and his party arrived in China now knows more about the People's Republic than he dared dreamed he would.

Thanks to our able TV correspondents, we are now aware of what a hat costs, what kind of leather people wear on the soles of their shoes, how people walk in a park, and how many bricks it takes to build a brick teahouse.

One can't help projecting into the future, when Mao Tse-tung makes his first visit to the United States and his activities are beamed back via satellite to the people in China:

"Good evening, comrades—this is Wo-pang of the Anti-Imperialist Television Network Broadcasting System, bringing to you live and in red color the banquet that President Nixon is giving in honor of our beloved and venerated leader, Chairman Mao, and his beloved and venerated wife, Madame Mao.

"Ba Ba Rah, what do you make of all of this so far?"

"Wo, the thing that impressed me the most was the reception the American people gave our beloved Mao. I was told by my interpreter that no one had received such a reception in Washington since Mayor John Lindsay joined the Democratic Party. The people seem very pleased to see Chairman Mao."

"Did you see many schoolchildren waving to Chairman Mao?"

"No, I didn't, but the interpreter told me that was because most of the children go to school on buses and it's hard to see them waving. Wo, what impressed you the most so far about this trip?"

"I think the thing that impressed me the most is that the U.S. Marine Band had managed to learn the Chinese national anthem. I believe this is a very good sign for future Chinese-American relations. They're starting to eat now. Do you have any idea what they're eating, Ba Ba Rah?"

"I have the menu right here in front of me. The first dish is fruit cocktail, which is supposed to be an American delicacy."

"It is, Ba Ba Rah. I had some for breakfast, and I can assure our Chinese viewers it is very delicious. Our beloved Mao is now eating his fruit salad with a spoon."

"Yes, Wo, Chairman Mao and Madame Mao have been practicing for months with a spoon and fork and knife. They both seem to be handling them very well."

"Quite well, Ba Ba Rah. Chairman Mao looks very much at ease. Who is that he is speaking to next to him?"

"My interpreter says that is Billy Graham, a minister who is the second-most-important man in the administration. The man speaking to Madame Mao is Bebe Rebozo, a friend of President Nixon's who is the third-most-important man in the administration."

"Chairman Mao is now talking to a woman. Who is she?"

"That is Martha Mitchell, who is considered the most important *woman* in the administration."

"Billy Graham seems to be handing pamphlets to Chairman Mao. What do you suppose they are?"

"I don't know, Wo, but my interpreter says he believes Mr. Graham may be trying to persuade Chairman Mao to become a Christian."

"Now Bebe Rebozo is handing pamphlets to Madame Mao. What do they say?"

"My interpreter says that Bebe Rebozo is probably trying to sell Madame Mao some Florida real estate."

"Who are those people who have just come out on the stage, Ba Ba Rah?"

"They are the American entertainers. They are called the Ray Conniff Singers."

"One of the women is pulling a sign out of her bosom. Is that unusual?"

"Oh, no, Wo. My interpreter informs me it is always done when somebody entertains at the White House."

MY SET IS BROKEN

It was two days after President Nixon's return from China, and the family went into the living room after dinner to watch television.

My wife turned on the set and said, "That's funny. There seems to be something wrong with the TV. I can't get Nixon on the tube."

"Try another channel," I suggested.

She switched to another channel and got a private-eye program. "He's not on this channel either."

I rose from my chair and started fiddling with the dials myself. I tried all the channels—no Nixon. "Who has been messing around with this set?" I shouted.

The kids were very defensive. "We didn't touch it," my son said.

My daughters also denied having done anything with it. "Damn it," I said, "we could turn on this set *any* time day or night on *any* channel and get a picture of Nixon. Now we can't even get him on educational TV."

"Maybe the cleaning woman did something wrong," my wife suggested. "I told her not to touch it."

Fuming, I called up my TV repairman, George Cury, and asked him to come over right away.

He asked if it could wait until the next day.

"Not on your life," I said. "I haven't missed Nixon on television in three years, and I'm not about to start tonight."

George came over with his tool kit. "I can't understand it," I said. "Nixon has been coming in loud and clear on prime time every evening. But tonight all I can get is a movie, Dean Martin, and a Lucy rerun."

Mr. Cury said, "Let me try." He flipped the dial back and forth. "You're right. There's something definitely wrong. Maybe it's in the aerial."

Mr. Cury climbed up on the roof and came back down. "The aerial seems to be all right. It's pointing toward China. You say you have had no trouble up until this week?"

"Right," I replied. "We watched his arrival at Andrews Air Force Base loud and clear in living color."

"Maybe it's in the tube," Mr. Cury said.

"What would a TV tube have to do with it?" I asked.

"Well, what happens is that when these tubes are installed, they emit a very strong Nixon signal, but as time goes on, the filament wears thin, the tube gets weaker and weaker. On some of the older sets people can't get Nixon at all. But this is a fairly new one, and you should be able to receive an image of Nixon even if it's only a shadow of himself."

Mr. Cury checked the tube and shook his head. "It's not there. Maybe there is something wrong with your horizontal adjuster. On some sets when Nixon starts fading from the screen, the trouble can be found with the horizontal dial. Tell me. The last time you saw Nixon was he standing up or lying down?"

"I think he was standing up," I said.

"Then maybe it's the vertical dial." Mr. Cury worked for three hours on the back of the set while we all waited nervously for him to fix it. Finally, he turned it on again. We got Dick Cavett, Johnny Carson, Perry Mason, and an old Wallace Beery movie. But still no Nixon.

Mr. Cury shook his head. "There's nothing I can do. You're going to have to throw away the TV."

"But it's only a year old," I protested.

"It's not my fault you got a lemon," he said. "It's obvious there is a weak Nixon fuse somewhere, but I can't find it."

"What will you give me on a trade-in?" I asked.

"Are you crazy?" he said. "For a set that can't even get Nixon in the daytime, I wouldn't give you a dime."

THE POEMS OF RICHARD NIXON

President Nixon was prepared for any emergency that might arise while he was in China. His staff had been working for months on every contingency the President might face. I can now reveal that the President, after hearing that Mao Tse-tung

writes poetry, was carrying poetry of his own in his briefcase to
read to Mao when the occasion presented itself. These are the
poems that Nixon could have sprung on Mao Tse-tung at any
time:

> If I must fly in a Chinese plane,
> will Air Force One be far behind?
>
> I stand at the Great Wall
> with Pat at my side.
> And as I breathe the centuries of history,
> the New Hampshire primary looks very small.
>
> There are no clouds in the sky,
> the wind is but a whisper in the trees,
> lakes sparkle as birds sing,
> it's a good day to bomb Cambodia.
>
> The journey of a thousand miles
> must begin with one single step.
> Unless you go to school
> and have to take a bus.
>
> Daybreak comes quietly,
> sneaking up on the dark.
> The sun finally commands the earth.
> I hope Kissinger had a good night.
>
> A dog barks; an eagle cries.
> The birds take flight;
> the deer stand frightened.
> I told them Phase II would work.
>
> The streams rush down from the mountain,
> washing the rocks with blue.
> The woods are filled with buds
> as spring wipes the frost from her eyes.
> I wonder if it's too early in the year
> to call a football coach.
>
> I made this journey into yesterday
> because I must think about tomorrow.
> If I should trip or lose my way,
> I'll deny it.

When I look at the universe, I am nothing.
When I look at a rose, I am nothing.
When I look at a newborn baby, I am nothing.
When I look at the ocean, I am nothing.
When I look at the polls, I am 49 percent.

As the sun sets over the Yellow River
and the moon rises in the China Sea,
I reach to the stars with both hands
knowing I will be on American TV.

KISSINGER'S STOMACHACHE

When the history books of this decade are written, they will
refer to Henry Kissinger's trip to China as "The Tummy Ache
Heard Round the World."

Using the excuse of an upset stomach, Mr. Kissinger
managed to elude everyone and high-tail it off to Peking to
have sweet-and-sour pork with Chou En-lai.

While it was a great ploy, Mr. Kissinger's "diplomatic
illness" could backfire on him. Suppose he *really* gets a
stomachache at some future time. Who is going to believe him?

Our scene opens in the medical room at the White House.
Henry staggers in, clutching his stomach, and says, "Doctor, I
have this pain right here."

The White House doctor laughs. "Good old Henry. Where
are you off to this time—the Suez Canal?"

"I'm not joking, Doc. It hurts terribly."

"I know," the doctor says. "The President is sending you to
talk to Castro."

Henry is now writhing on the floor. "Believe me, it hurts.
Right in the gut. You see, I had dinner with Gloria Steinem and
Bella Abzug, and they served me Bon Vivant vichyssoise. Since
I was out of the country at the time, I didn't know you weren't
supposed to eat it."

"You really can put on an act, Henry. I wouldn't be surprised
if you turned up in Albania next week."

Henry crawls out of the doctor's office on his hands and
knees.

Ron Ziegler, the President's press secretary, sees him crawling down the hall.

"Hello, Mr. Kissinger," Ron says. "Can I help you?"

"Get me to a hospital."

Ron takes out his notebook. "That's a good cover story. I'll announce you were taken to a hospital this morning. I won't tell them which hospital."

"No, Ron, I don't want you to announce I was taken to a hospital. I want you to get me to a hospital."

Ron winks at him. "Is it East Berlin or Yalta?"

"Please, Ron. I'm sick. I'm going to die."

"I doubt if the press corps would buy that, Mr. Kissinger. If we announce that you've died, and then you pop up at San Clemente a week later, the newspaper guys will get awfully mad. Let me announce you're having your tonsils out. I have to go to my press briefing now. I'll see you later."

Henry is rolling on the floor as Secretary of State William Rogers comes by.

"Hello, Henry. You going to the Cabinet meeting?"

"Mr. Secretary, my stomach. I have a pain in my stomach. It's killing me."

Secretary Rogers says angrily, "Well, no one has informed me about it. What are you up to this time?"

"I'm not up to anything, Mr. Secretary. Could you call an ambulance?"

"Hanoi," Rogers says. "You're cooking up something in Hanoi. I'll probably be the last one to know about it."

"I'm not going to Hanoi. I'm really sick."

"No kidding? Well, I'm sorry to hear that, Henry." And Rogers smiles and walks away.

With his last ounce of strength, Henry staggers into the Oval Room and falls down in front of the President.

"Henry," the President says. "You don't have to prostrate yourself in front of me. I know you're loyal."

Henry is in such agony he can't speak.

"What is it, Henry?" the President says. "Would you like to go to Morocco?"

Henry shakes his head.

"The Vatican? You want to see the Pope?"

Henry groans.

The President gets up. "I don't have time to play games, Henry. Write me a memo telling me what you want. By the way, Mrs. Nixon said she would like you for dinner tonight. We're having meat loaf."

Henry screams and passes out, as the curtain falls.

IV. HOW IS EVERYTHING
IN PARANOIA?

HURTS RENT-A-GUN

The Senate recently passed a new gun-control bill, which some observers consider worse than no bill at all. Any serious attempt at handgun registration was gutted, and Senate gun lovers even managed to repeal a 1968 gun law controlling the purchase of .22 rimfire ammunition.

After the Senate got finished with its work on the gun-control bill, I received a telephone call from my friend Bromley Hurts, who told me he had a business proposition to discuss with me. I met him for lunch at a pistol range in Maryland.

"I think I've got a fantastic idea," he said. "I want to start a new business called Hurts Rent-A-Gun."

"What on earth for?" I asked.

"There are a lot of people in this country who only use a handgun once or twice a year, and they don't want to go to all the expense of buying one. So we'll rent them a gun for a day or two. By leasing a firearm from us, they won't have to tie up all their money."

"That makes sense," I admitted.

"Say a guy is away from home on a trip, and he doesn't want to carry his own gun with him. He can rent a gun from us and then return it when he's finished with his business."

"You could set up rent-a-gun counters at gas stations," I said excitedly.

"And we could have stores in town where someone could rent a gun to settle a bet," Hurts said.

"A lot of people would want to rent a gun for a domestic quarrel," I said.

"Right. Say a jealous husband suspects there is someone at home with his wife. He rents a pistol from us and tries to catch them in the act. If he discovers his wife is alone, he isn't out the eighty dollars it would have cost him to buy a gun."

"Don't forget about kids who want to play Russian roulette. They could pool their allowances and rent a gun for a couple of hours," I said.

"Our market surveys indicate," Hurts said, "that there are also a lot of kids who claim their parents don't listen to them. If they could rent a gun, they feel they could arrive at an understanding with their folks in no time."

"There's no end to the business," I said. "How would you charge for Hurts Rent-A-Gun?"

"There would be hourly rates, day rates, and weekly rates, plus ten cents for each bullet fired. Our guns would be the latest models, and we would guarantee clean barrels and the latest safety devices. If a gun malfunctions through no fault of the user, we will give him another gun absolutely free."

"For many Americans it's a dream come true," I said.

"We've also made it possible for people to return the gun in another town. For example, if you rent the gun in Chicago and want to use it in Salt Lake City, you can drop it off there at no extra charge."

"Why didn't you start this before?"

"We wanted to see what happened with the gun-control legislation. We were pretty sure the Senate and the White House would not do anything about strong gun control, especially during an election year. But we didn't want to invest a lot of money until we were certain they would all chicken out."

"I'd like the franchise for Washington's National Airport," I said.

"You've got it. It's a great location," Hurts said. "You'll make a fortune in hijackings alone."

DON'T CALL IT POT

Drug hearings were held in Washington not long ago. Several doctors testified that many of the drugs sold over the counter are useless and in some cases harmful. Those billions the American public spends on patent medicine remedies, according to testimony, are just thrown down the drain.

Will anything be done about this? Not while the drug lobby is alive and well in Washington.

Which brings up the subject of pot.

Malcolm Ruddemaker, a friend (attention all narc agents—I made up his name, so don't ask me to reveal who he is before a grand jury), told me, "The trouble with pot is that it was introduced to the American public under the wrong auspices. The counterculture thought they could go it alone, and in so doing they brought down the wrath of the courts and the legislators on their heads."

"I don't understand."

"Because of the counterculture's suspicion of big business, they tried to cut out the middleman. When you do that in the United States, you are in for a lot of trouble."

"You mean if you had gotten the giant American companies interested in marijuana from the beginning, we wouldn't be sending kids off to jail?"

"Exactly. Suppose the kids, instead of growing and marketing their own pot, had gone to one of the big drug companies and said, 'We know how you can make fifty million dollars a year.' What kind of response do you think they would have gotten?"

"Well, I know the drug company wouldn't have thrown them out of the office," I said.

"You bet your sweet prescription they wouldn't. The first thing they would ask the kids is, 'What exactly do you have on your minds?'

"The kids would reply, 'We have this drug which relieves tension, relaxes you, makes you sleep better, and takes away aches and pains in minutes.'

" 'Is it a pill?'

" 'No,' the kids would reply, 'it's a cigarette. You just take a few drags on a butt, and it does the same work as any two pills.'

" *'Caramba!'* the drug people would say. 'What do you call it?' The kids would reply, 'Pot.'

" 'That's a terrible name,' the drug people would say. 'We must call it something like Relax-A-Lot and advertise it as Mother Nature's Own Tranquilizer.'

" 'We don't care what you call it,' the kids would say, 'just as long as we can buy it in a drugstore.' "

"And you think the drug company would market it?" I asked Ruddemaker.

"In a flash—with a multimillion-dollar media campaign to back it up," he replied.

"But wouldn't the government stop them from making it?" I asked.

"Are you kidding? The government is not going to mess around with a big legitimate drug company that has friends in the Senate, the House, *and* the White House.

"Besides, other companies would bring out their own versions of Relax-A-Lot, and then the government would have to deal with the drug lobby as well. You're talking about big political campaign contributions now."

"I hadn't thought of that. If only the kids had used their heads, they wouldn't be in all this trouble about pot."

"It's never too late," Ruddemaker said. "I think the kids should turn over all their pot rights to the drug industry and say, 'You guys market it. We'd like to get out of sales.' In no time the American people who are fighting marijuana use would be lining up at drug counters all over the country screaming for fast, fast relief."

THE TROUBLE WITH HARRY

I recently received a call from a guy who claimed he was president of the Harry Anti-Defamation League. He said, "You wrote an article last week in which you used the name Harry to make fun of a TV football situation. For years now radio, television, and newspaper writers have been holding up the name Harry to ridicule and derision, and we Harrys have banned together to do something about it."

"Now wait a minute, sir," I protested. "I do not always use Harry when I need a fall guy. Sometimes I use George, other times Arnie, and quite often I use Henry."

"That's what I mean," Harry said. "Why don't you ever make fun of the Steves or Jims or Jacks or Bills?"

"There is nothing funny about a Steve, a Jim, a Jack or a Bill," I answered frankly. "The image just isn't right. If I call my guy Chuck or Jack, my reader is going to expect him to punch someone in the nose. But if I call him Harry or Fred or Louie, the reader is going to expect him to *be* punched in the nose. It's as simple as that."

"But why should this be? We Harrys and Mortons and Arnies and Chesters have a right to live, too."

"I didn't make the rules," I protested. "A long time ago there must have been a Harry who slipped on a banana peel. From then on, any time a writer needed a name for someone who was going to get all fouled up, he used Harry."

"Well, we Harrys don't like it," Harry said. "It's bad enough that people are always making fun of Harry, but it's even worse when they make him the guy who commits the crime on a TV show."

"I don't know why you take offense at that," I said. "Everyone knows that if a Harry doesn't have two left feet, he probably has criminal instincts."

"Yeah, but why does a Harry always have to be one of Rocco's boys or Frank's henchmen? Why can't he be the leader of the mob?"

"People just don't think of Harry as a leader," I said. "Writers know this. If they have to come up with a name for a gang leader, they would rather go with Red or Dusty or even Phil. You just can't see a Harry being the brains behind a bank job. As a matter of fact, it's more likely that he's the guy to make the fatal error so everyone gets caught."

"You see? All your prejudices about Harrys are coming through. Those of us who are not public jokes are stool pigeons."

"Not necessarily," I said. "Max is more liable to rat on the gang than Harry."

"We aren't taking it anymore," Harry said. "From now on every time we see a Harry presented in a bad light on television, we're going to call the sponsor and tell him that everyone in this country named Harry is going to boycott his product. And we also intend to cancel our subscriptions to any newspaper that holds up a Harry to derision."

"Frankly, sir . . ." I began.

"The name's Harry," he said angrily.

"Harry, then," I said. "I think you're being oversensitive. If your name was Hubert or Alfred or even Bert, you might have a case. But I only use Harry when I'm looking for a minor schnook. If I'm looking for a real hopeless case, I'll never use Harry."

"Who do you use then?"

"Marvin."

WHILE SANTA WATCHES

Santa Claus was sitting in front of his television set on Christmas Eve watching the Redskin-Green Bay Packers play-off game when Mrs. Claus came in.

"Are you going to sit there all day watching that idiotic football game?"

"Will you get out of here and leave me alone?" Santa Claus said.

"But you've got to go to work. The sleigh is piled high with toys, and the reindeer are getting very impatient."

"Listen, this play-off means a lot to me. If the reindeer are cold, they can come in and watch the game with me."

"How can you behave that way? Children all over the world are waiting for you to come down their chimneys tonight. You'll never make it if you don't start now," Mrs. Claus said.

Santa opened another can of beer. "For heaven's sake, woman, can't I relax for a few hours without your yakking at me?"

"If you don't deliver those toys, they're going to find a new Santa Claus and you're going to be out of a job."

Santa took a swallow. "How did I know they were going to have a play-off game on Christmas Eve? Answer me that! If I had known it, I would have made my deliveries yesterday."

"Yesterday was not Christmas Eve!" Mrs. Claus screamed. "Look at you sitting there in your undershirt, swilling beer, with your fat stomach sticking out. You certainly have the holiday spirit."

"There goes Larry Brown!" Santa yelled. "A twelve-yard gain. Now there's a football player."

"You're not even listening to me. Will you get dressed and get on that stupid sled and go to work?"

"Not until the game is over," Santa said. "I can work any day, but how often do the Redskins get into a play-off game? Do you have any more potato chips to go with this beer?"

"Don't you understand Christmas won't be Christmas if you don't get those toys distributed? Just think—tomorrow morning millions and millions of children will come downstairs with their hearts beating fast, excitement glistening in their eyes, knees trembling—and what will they find? Nothing. Why? Because Santa Claus was sitting on his fat butt watching a football game."

"That's easy for you to say," Santa said. "But I've been sitting here Sunday after Sunday, not to mention Monday nights, rooting for the Redskins. And now that they've made it and are in a play-off for the Super Bowl, you want me to leave them in the lurch to deliver a bunch of toys on the coldest day of the year. A man has to have priorities. Be quiet. This could be a crucial play."

"All right," said Mrs. Claus, "if you won't leave the T-V set, *I'll* deliver the toys."

"But you don't like to drive a sleigh in icy weather."

Mrs. Claus threw on an overcoat, put on boots, and wrapped a scarf around her head. "It doesn't matter. I'm not going to have those children disappointed."

"Okay," Santa shrugged. "Here's the list. Be careful going over Detroit. It gets very smoggy this time of the year."

Mrs. Claus grabbed the list, stomped out, and slammed the door. Santa passed a beer to one of his elves. "Women sure get mad when they see a man enjoying himself. Ho! Ho! Ho!"

SHOULD CHURCHES STAY OPEN?

One of the big questions confronting the country is "Should the churches be allowed to remain open on Christmas Day?"

A group of citizens have banned together to protest the way churches are trying to turn Christmas into a religious holiday.

Wendell Wankel, their spokesman, said, "If we allow the churches to do business on Christmas Day, the holiday will lose all its commercial meaning.

"We believe that Christmas is a time for gift giving and eating and television watching, and anything that interferes should be forbidden."

"But," I protested, "there are some people who would like to go to church on Christmas Day. Surely you don't want to interfere with that?"

"They can go to church on Sunday or during the week. Why do they insist on going the one day of the year when people should stay home and enjoy the fruits of our great economy?"

"Maybe they want to thank God for all the good things He has brought them," I suggested.

"That's not enough of a reason to keep the churches open," Wankel said. "Look at all the traffic congestion it causes. The church bells wake up people who are trying to sleep late. Besides, why shouldn't priests and ministers have a day off like everybody else?"

"Maybe they like to work on Christmas."

"That's not the point," Wankel said. "If you keep the churches open, you detract from the great materialistic fervor in this country. We say religion has its place, but not at Christmas."

"But," I said, "Christmas *once* was a religious holiday."

"When?" Wankel asked.

"Quite a few years ago. I read a book that said at one time the religious aspect of Christmas was more important than the exchanging of gifts."

"I don't believe you," Wankel said.

"It's true. The original idea of Christmas was to celebrate the birth of Christ."

"You read that in a book?" he asked disbelievingly.

"Yup. Serious gift giving didn't take place in this country until the department stores got into it. Before that, people gave their children toys and went to church. In some communities going to church was the highlight of Christmas Day."

"I'd like to see that book," Wankel said suspiciously. "Anyway that was another era, and we're dealing with *today*. Our main point is that if you keep churches open, people will feel a temptation to go to them. Entire families may wind up there, and this could hurt the ski-resort business very badly."

"I respect your feelings about Christmas, Wankel," I said, "but I don't think any group in the United States should dictate to any other group what houses of worship must remain open or closed on Christmas."

Wankel replied, "Too much time, money, and advertising have gone into Christmas to have a small minority spoil it by going to church. We're not against churches per se. We're just against churches remaining open on the one day of the year that is sacred to our gross national product."

"Suppose, in spite of your protests, the churches still remain open on Christmas Day. What will you do?"

Wankel smiled. "God will show us a way."

WEATHER THOU GOEST

Something is happening to the weather in this country, and it's causing tremendous anxiety amongst the people. In the days before television, nobody really cared *that* much about weather. You got up in the morning and looked out the window. If it was raining, you put on rubbers; if it was snowing, you put on boots. If it was a lousy day, you always figured that tomorrow the sun would shine.

But now, thanks to the miracle of television, people worry about the weather all the time. We are told not only what weather to expect in our neck of the woods, but also what's happening in Billings, Montana, and Pitchfork, Newfoundland.

This not only causes traumas in most American households, but also polarizes the country.

For example, the other night a group of friends were watching the weather on the local news. The jolly newscaster was standing in front of a map of the North American continent chuckling as he informed us that we could expect rain, sleet, and fog for the next forty-eight hours. Had he let it go at that, nobody would have been too upset, but he decided to go into a long explanation about what caused it.

Using his pointer he said, "As you can see, there is a mass of cold air coming in from Canada. . . ."

"Canada always keeps sending us cold masses of air," my friend Harry Dalinsky said. "If Nixon has any guts, he'll tell them to knock it off or else."

"Or else what?" Collins Bird asked.

"We'll send them masses of cold air that will make their masses of cold air look like a trade wind," Dalinsky said.

"I wouldn't fool with Canada when it comes to cold air masses," Bird said. "They have a cold air superiority over us of five to one."

The announcer continued his chalk talk.

"This cold air mass from Canada is expected to meet with this warm air mass coming up from the South, which will cause the rain, sleet, and fog that will arrive in our area tomorrow morning."

"There is your problem," said Carey Winston. "It isn't cold air coming from Canada that is causing the trouble; it's the warm air from the South. They shouldn't allow the South to send up any warm air at the same time Canada is sending down cold air."

"Nixon isn't going to make the South stop sending up warm air, not after what they did for him during the election," Jim Symington said.

"He has always maintained," Dalinsky agreed, "that the exporting of warm air should be left to the individual states."

The weatherman was still talking away. "The Midwest can expect heavy snow, which is blowing in from the Rockies."

"I'll bet you the people in the Midwest are really mad at the Rockies," Collins Bird said.

"They shouldn't have settled so near the Rockies," Carey Winston said. "I have no sympathy for them."

"Why do you say that?" I asked.

"Because the Midwest sends us all their bad weather. They get furious because they have all that snow dumped on them, so they want to dump it on someone else," Winston replied. "I'll start feeling sorry for people who live in the Middle West when they stop dropping their snow on us."

The announcer continued. "The thunderstorms are expected in Texas and Oklahoma."

"They'll probably get a tax depletion allowance for them," Symington said.

"Now," said the weatherman, "let's look at our satellite map of the United States. As you can see, there is a cloud cover over the entire United States except for Key Biscayne, Florida, where the President is spending his holidays."

My wife said, "It figures."

MAFIA, INC.

The Mafia is becoming one of the major industries in the United States. Every book on the Mafia sells like hot cakes. *The*

Godfather is expected to gross more than $100,000,000. Even a lousy film like *The Valachi Papers* is cleaning up at the box office. The American people seem to have an insatiable appetite for any book, film, TV show, or newspaper article on the mob.

The only one that has not cashed in on this Mafia mania is the mob itself and this has caused a great deal of consternation among the members of the "families" throughout the United States. A meeting was called last month at the Loew's Cosa Nostra in upstate New York to see if something could be done.

Salvatore Mastrella of the New England family said, "All the book publishers, newspapers, and movie companies have been making a fortune out of us. We're supposed to be smart guys, and we're getting ripped off by everyone. This is 'our thing,' and we haven't made a dime on it."

Joseph Fanatelli, the don of the California Mafia, said, "You can say that again. They're exploiting us.

"We risk our necks in numbers, dope and prostitution and some straight guy sells our story to a publisher for five hundred thousand dollars. And they don't even send us a free book."

Mastrella said, "It's about time the syndicate started to cash in on the Mafia craze in the country. Now this is my plan. We have to have our own literary department."

"Thatsa great idea," said Joey "Cement Feet" Magino of Buffalo. "How do we do it?"

"First," said Mastrella, "we set up a corporation called Mafia Enterprises. We copyright the name so no one can use it without our permission. Then we start offering books written by our own people to the publishers. We tell them, 'You want a book on the Mafia, we'll give you a book on the Mafia.' It will be straight from the horse's mouth. Then they give us a contract."

"A contract?" Flat Nose Gambollo of the Bronx family said. "We going to put a contract out on the publisher?"

"No, you stupid jerk," Mastrella said. "A contract is a signed piece of paper saying the publisher will pay us for the book."

"I never heard of a contract like that," Gambollo said.

Mastrella ignored him. "Now we keep the movie rights, the pocketbook rights, the TV rights, and the sweat-shirt rights. If they want to make a movie of the book they have to come to us. We sell the movie rights for a million dollars and provide technical advisers for a thousand dollars a day."

"I gotta question," said Don Fanatelli. "Suppose we gotta book about the Mafia and the Bronx family sells their book to the movies first. How we gonna worka that out?"

Mastrella said, "That's a good question. We divide the country up. The New York family deals with Paramount, the Detroit family deals with MGM, the New England family can sell their story only to Columbia Pictures, the California family works with Twentieth Century-Fox, and the New Orleans family sells their movie rights to Walt Disney."

"Hey!" Carlo Longo of New Orleans said. "Walt Disney don't do no Mafia pictures."

"Thatsa your problem, Longo. You have to make them an offer they can't refuse."

Fanatelli said, "I like the plan. As a matter of fact, my wife has been wanting me to write my story for a long time now. She says it's better than any fiction she's read."

Mastrella said, "Okay, it's agreed upon. When we leave here, we go to our typewriters. And I don't want any messy manuscripts. Publishers like neatness. And no stealing each other's stories. Any guy who gets caught swiping another mob's anecdotes is automatically a candidate for the Corpse-of-the-Month Club."

A GREAT HONOR

The worst thing that can happen to any public official in this country is to be mentioned for a top appointment in the government and not get it.

It isn't just the rejection of the job that is hard to swallow—it is that while he is under consideration, the candidate is being subjected to exhaustive investigation by everyone from the FBI to the *Harvard Law Review*, and his reputation can be destroyed forever.

The Supreme Court nomination circus that President Nixon

put on is a perfect example of how dangerous it is to be mentioned for one of the highest positions in the land.

Take the case of Judge Chilblain Clamchowder. Judge Clamchowder, who had been appointed to the Fifth Circuit Traffic Court for the work he had done in carrying Tornado County for President Nixon in 1968, found himself listed as one of the "leading" candidates for a Supreme Court seat.

Judge Clamchowder told me in his chambers, "I knew they had just thrown in my name as a smoke screen, and at first I was flattered to see my name in the newspapers.

"But then the Eastern Establishment press started coming down here and asking about me, and my life has become pure hell.

"They talked to my second wife, who said I had cheated not only on her, but also on my bar exam. Even if it's true, it's something you don't like to read about in the newspapers."

Judge Clamchowder continued: "Then some Democratic Senators found out I hadn't paid my income tax for the past five years, and they tried to make a big deal of it just to embarrass the Nixon administration. They made it sound as if I was the first Supreme Court Justice nominee who had ever cheated on his taxes.

"To make matters worse, the FBI discovered that I was a major stockholder in the firm that prints all the traffic tickets for Tornado County. So I had to get rid of the stock at a great financial sacrifice.

"Then Jack Anderson found out about a Christmas party I had last year in my chambers for the meter maids, and while only two of them took off their clothes, he made it sound like an orgy. So now my third wife is suing me for divorce, and it's gonna be damn expensive, particularly since I don't have an interest in the printing firm any more.

"The American Civil Liberties Union then dug up the fact that I had donated a thousand dollars to buy dynamite to blow up all the school buses in Tornado County, and that made the newspaper headlines. Now I believe this was a personal matter and had nothing to do with whether a person would make a good Supreme Court justice or not.

"Finally, some smart-aleck law professor discovered that

since I've been ruling on traffic offenses, I have been reversed by higher courts seven hundred and sixty-eight times.

"He also claimed I had fixed the tickets of forty-five members of my country club. It turns out I had only fixed forty tickets since I've been on the traffic court, but the media doesn't seem to be concerned with accuracy as long as it's a good story.

"The American Bar Association rated me as 'less mediocre,' and this certainly hasn't helped me keep any decorum in the courtroom."

"From what I can tell, Judge," I said, "you might have done better by not being mentioned as a possible Supreme Court Justice."

"Frankly," he replied, "if it wasn't for the honor, I would just as soon forget it."

CHRISTMAS PHASE II

There were many persons concerned with how Phase II would affect their Christmas. Here are some letters the Cost of Living Council had to deal with.

The first is from a man named Ebenezer Scrooge, a partner in the firm of Scrooge and Marley. Mr. Scrooge wrote:

DEAR SIR,

I have an employee named Bob Cratchit who works as a clerk in my warehouse. For some years I was under the impression that Cratchit was not doing his share of the work. (For example, he always asked to take Christmas Day off, which I have considered humbug.)

But last year I had a bad experience. I won't go into the details, other than to say it changed my attitude on many things. One of them was my feeling toward Cratchit. I decided I had been mistaken about him, and to make amends, I promised him a raise. Unfortunately, I told him the raise would go into effect on August 16, 1971.

My question is: Can I now go ahead and give him this raise, as I would hate to go through the same bad trip this Christmas as I did last year?

Scrooge's letter was turned over to someone at the pay board, who replied:

DEAR MR. SCROOGE,
Your letter in regard to your employee Robert Cratchit was referred to this office. Unfortunately, we cannot give you a definite answer at this time as to whether you can raise his salary. The raise, if permitted, would have to be within the wage guidelines set forth by the Cost of Living Council.
Would you be kind enough to tell us if this is a merit raise, an across-the-board raise, or an inflationary raise which would cause you to raise the price of your products?
Speaking for the administration, we urge you to forgo Mr. Cratchit's raise at this time so that we all can win the President's great battle against inflation.

Another sample of the kind of mail the Cost of Living Council got comes from Mrs. Della Young, who wrote:

We have no money for Christmas this year so I'm going to sell my beautiful hair and with it buy a gold chain for my husband's watch. I understand Jim is secretly planning to sell his watch to buy a comb for my beautiful hair. Are we permitted to do this under Mr. Nixon's Phase II economic plan?

DEAR MRS. YOUNG,
In answer to your question, I am advised to tell you that you can exchange a gold watch-chain for a comb, provided you apply for an exemption on combs and watch-chains as specified in Paragraph 4A, Chapter XII of Volume III of Phase II price and wage guidelines (as amended in Index 345). Please submit in quadruplicate your request to the price commission and we will try to get you an answer before March 1, 1972.

The final letter came from a young girl named Virginia.

DEAR SIR,
Is there a Santa Claus? My friends say that under Phase II there isn't. Who am I to believe?

DEAR VIRGINIA,

You should stop speaking to people like George Meany and get on the President's team.

Hail to the Chief,
SECRETARY OF THE TREASURY

V. APATHY LANDSLIDE

TV COMMERCIALS FOR CANDIDATES

Some of the political television commercials that appear on our television screens are pretty boring; others are rather tough on the opponents.

It seems to me that the men in charge of making up advertising campaigns for our Presidential candidates would have done just as well if they had taken the TV commercials that were on the air and paraphrased them for their own use.

For example, I could see Pat Nixon cooking a steak over a campfire. She says to the audience, "I've been First Lady for quite a number of years, and yet I feel younger now than when Dick first took the job as President. That's because I exercise, get eight hours' sleep, eat right, and take iron for my blood. Dick treats me better now than he did when I used to wear a cloth coat."

Just then we see Richard Nixon walking toward Pat. He's dressed in a plaid wool shirt and blue jeans. He comes behind her and kisses her on the neck. Then he says to the camera, "My wife, I think I'll keep her."

Another one could have shown Senator George McGovern
and his wife in their home.

McGovern says, "I don't feel like going out and campaigning
today. I just seem so sluggish and tired these days."

Eleanor looks at him and asks, "Is it . . . uhhh . . .
irregularity?"

McGovern nods his head sheepishly.

"I have just the thing for it." She holds up a blue bottle.

We cut to McGovern at a rally. He's smiling and happy. The
crowds are cheering. He hugs Eleanor and says, "I feel great,
thanks to you."

Eleanor giggles. ". . . and Snow White Formula 67."

Another commercial could have shown Spiro Agnew on the
golf course playing with Arnie Palmer. Then the camera cuts to
the country club locker room. "That was great fun," Agnew
says as he takes off his shirt. "I wish I didn't have to go out now
and face those rotten, miserable kids. They hate me. I can't
understand why."

Arnie Palmer says, "Maybe it has something to do with
underarm perspiration."

Agnew says, "But I use a deodorant."

"Yes," says Arnie, holding up a can, "but maybe you need a
dry one that lasts all day. When you're out campaigning, most
deodorants won't give you twenty-four-hour protection."
Agnew takes the can from Arnie.

We cut to Agnew on a college campus. A group of kids, all
with beards and wearing beads, are crowded around him, and
they're laughing. "We want Spiro! We want Spiro!" they start
chanting. Then Agnew turns to the camera and winks. "Arnie
was right. All deodorants aren't alike."

The final commercial idea could have shown Sarge Shriver.
First he's eating a pizza in an Italian neighborhood; then he's
eating a frankfurter in a Jewish delicatessen; then he's eating
Polish ham in a Polish restaurant; then he's eating an Idaho
potato on a farm.

Then we cut to Sarge in bed with Eunice. He's groaning and
moaning, "I can't believe I ate the. . . ."

"Don't say it!" Eunice screams as she jumps out of bed and

rushes to the medicine cabinet. She gives him two tablets in a glass of water.

The next morning Sarge, refreshed and sparkling, says to Eunice, "Well, I've got to go to a catfish fry at the All Souls Baptist Church this morning, so just give me some of your delicious scrambled eggs, bacon, and an English muffin for breakfast."

Eunice puts her arms around Sarge's neck and smiles into the camera. "My husband, I think I'll keep him."

HANDLING GOP FUNDS

The Republicans seemed to be having some problem explaining how they collected donations for the party. The General Accounting Office (GAO) accused the party of mishandling their campaign funds, to which the Committee for the Reelection of the President replied, "Nonsense!"

The trouble seems to be that the GAO and the Democrats don't understand how the Republicans processed their money. If they did, there would be no question of impropriety.

This is how the system worked:

When someone gave a $25,000 donation in the form of a check to the Committee for the Reelection of the President, a party official was sent to pick it up. He then cashed the check at a bank in Houston.

Another official picked up the cash and flew it to Portland, Maine, where it was placed in a safe in the office of a Lawyer for Nixon.

After a week the money was taken out of the safe by another Republican official, who took it to Wall Street and purchased a cashier's check with it.

The cashier's check was turned over to a public relations man, who carried it to Minneapolis and handed it to a courier, who flew the check to Seattle, where it was cashed and used to buy short-term municipal notes at 6 percent.

These notes were then placed in a special bra of a Republican national committeewoman, who flew to San Francisco.

The Republican committeewoman turned the notes over to Governor Ronald Reagan's chauffeur, who drove to Los Angeles and delivered them to John Wayne's business manager.

He took them to the First National Bank of San Clemente, where he cashed them. The cash was handed to a close friend of Maurice Stans, who buried the money in a cigar box in his backyard under an avocado tree.

A week later, at midnight, Frank Sinatra and Efrem Zimbalist, Jr., dug up the box and flew it to Palm Springs, where it was turned over to a caddie on the eighth hole of the Thunderbird golf course.

The cash was then converted into diamonds, which were placed in the false bottom of a suitcase, taken by Sammy Davis, Jr., to New Orleans, and placed in an old grandfather clock on the plantation of a Democrat for Nixon.

Two weeks later the diamonds were removed from their hiding place and converted into soybean futures. The soybean futures were then sold for ITT bonds at 8 percent. These bonds were taken by Greyhound bus to El Paso, where they were placed in a waterproof packet and turned over to a frogman, who swam the Rio Grande with them on his back.

A Mexican for Nixon, on horseback, picked up the packet on the other side of the river and rode to Mexico City, where the bonds were cashed for pesos. The pesos were placed in a bank.

Two weeks later a bank in Miami sent a draft to the bank in Mexico City for $25,000. The money was cabled to Miami, where it was put into the bank account of a former CIA man.

The money remained in the account until someone in Washington wired the CIA man to give the cash to a Cuban refugee.

The Cuban refugee then took the money and used it to pay outstanding bills for the Republicans, including those for bumper stickers, buttons, outdoor billboard signs, and TV spot commercials.

There are probably easier ways for the Republicans to handle their financial contributions, but so far they haven't been able to come up with any.

"But," a Republican finance man assured us, "we're working on it."

THE UNDECIDED VOTER

It was election day, and Stieglitz, who was undecided on how he was going to vote, woke up at seven o'clock. His wife asked him what he wanted for breakfast.

"I don't know," Stieglitz said.

"Do you want eggs or do you want cereal?"

"I like eggs," Stieglitz said, "but I also enjoy cereal."

"Well, what about pancakes?"

"I hadn't thought of pancakes," Stieglitz said. "That really does make the choice hard."

"Would you please make up your mind?" Stieglitz's wife asked.

"Let's see. Eggs, cereal, or pancakes? You forgot waffles."

"Do you want waffles?"

"I don't think so."

Stieglitz's wife brought him a cup of coffee and a hard roll.

After breakfast they got into his car to go to the voting polls at the local public school.

"How are you going to get there?" Stieglitz's wife asked.

"If I go down Foxhall Road, I'll run into a lot of traffic. But if I go down MacArthur Boulevard, I'll hit a lot of lights."

"Do you want me to drive?" Stieglitz's wife asked.

"That's an interesting question," Stieglitz said. "I don't mind driving, yet if you drove, I wouldn't have to decide which way I wanted to go to the public school. Yet I don't see why you should drive since it's my car. But then again, you've driven my car before. Of course, you haven't driven it when we were going to vote."

"Oh, for heaven's sakes!" Stieglitz's wife screamed. "Will you do something?"

Stieglitz started the car.

As they arrived at the public school, they discovered many other voters had arrived already, and Stieglitz had a difficult time finding a place to park.

"What about over there?" his wife suggested, pointing out a space next to the playground.

"It looks like a good spot," Stieglitz agreed. "But maybe after I park there, somebody will park behind me and I'll have difficulty pulling out."

"Well, park over there behind the red car."

"I could park over there, but then I might be sorry I didn't park by the playground."

"What are you going to do?"

"I think I'll drive around the block a few times. Then someone will take one of the spots, and I'll have no choice but to take the other."

Stieglitz finally parked, and he and his wife walked into the school. The lady behind the table gave Stieglitz a slip of paper. "You may go to any one of the three booths that are empty."

"Any one of the three?"

"Yes, they're all alike. It doesn't make any difference which one you vote in."

Stieglitz just stood there and stared.

"Please, sir," the lady said, "you're holding up the line."

"I don't know which booth to go into," Stieglitz said.

"All right, go into the first one."

"Why not the second or the third one?" Stieglitz demanded. "You said they were all alike."

"All right, go into the second or third one if you want to."

"Why not the first one?"

The lady called over a policeman. "Harry, we've got another undecided voter over here."

The policeman came over and said, "Okay, Mac, I've had it up to here with you people. You get your tail in one of those booths and pull the lever or I'll split your skull!"

"Pull the lever?" Stieglitz asked. "Up or down?"

AN APATHY LANDSLIDE

APATHY WINS IN LANDSLIDE! was the headline in the morning's newspapers.

I went to Apathy's hotel headquarters in hopes of interviewing the winner, but his aides said he was resting.

"Did he have a tough night?" I asked.

"No, he's always resting. He sleeps a lot."

Refusing to be put off, I sneaked up to his room and, without knocking, walked in. Apathy was lying on his bed in his underwear.

"I'm sorry to break in on you," I said apologetically.

Apathy yawned. "I couldn't care less."

"You apparently are the big winner in this election. How do you feel about it?"

"All right, I guess. I really didn't care if I won or not. Frankly, I don't feel any different now from the way I did before the race."

"That's interesting," I said, writing very fast. "What made you enter the campaign in the first place?"

"I was drafted," Apathy said. "Early in the year the pollsters and pundits indicated there was tremendous grass-roots support for Apathy in this country. It started when people suddenly realized they might have four more years of Nixon. Then McGovern was nominated in Miami, and that put the clincher on it. People came to me and said, 'Apathy, this is your year.' Well, I didn't have anything else to do, so I agreed to run."

"And you did well," I said. "Can you tell me a little about the strategy you used?"

"My strategy was not to do *anything*. I let McGovern campaign on TV, I let Nixon campaign on radio, and I let Agnew and Shriver go all over the country. The more exposure they had the more Apathetic the country became. By election day I was seventy-five points ahead in the polls."

"But surely you did something to lull the country into a false sense of complacency."

"I'm not being modest when I say I didn't make a speech, issue a statement, or spend one cent on my campaign. But I got all the press. The columnists and the commentators kept talking about Apathy in this campaign every day. Wherever people gathered to discuss the election, Apathy was the first thing mentioned. Both parties were knocking themselves out for their candidates, but I was the one who got all the exposure."

"I imagine," I said, "you became very nervous when the Watergate bugging scandal broke."

"My staff panicked; they wanted me to do something about it. They were afraid the American people would lose their Apathy after that. But I just told them to sit tight. I knew it was impossible to get the American people shook up about anything anymore. And I was right. No matter what came out on the Watergate, the electorate stayed Apathetic, and I didn't lose a vote."

"Was there any time during the campaign when you felt you were in trouble?"

"The only time I had a scare was when technicians striking against CBS cut the cables before the New York Jets-Washington Redskins game on Sunday.

"For the first time everyone in the country was aroused and lost their Apathy, and I was afraid they would remain infuriated until election day. But CBS gave them all another football game to watch, and everybody went back to sleep."

"Apparently you've been given a mandate by the American people. What do you intend to do with it?"

"Nothing," Apathy said. "If I did anything, I'd just shake people up."

Mrs. Apathy came into the bedroom in her slip, drinking a can of beer.

"How does it feel to be the First Lady of the land?" I asked her.

She shrugged and took a sip from the can. "Beats the hell out of me."

GUESS WHO'S COMING TO DINNER?

The political campaign was under way, and some wild promises by the Presidential and Vice Presidential candidates were expected.

Sargent Shriver told the people of West Virginia that if

George McGovern were elected, the poor people would be eating in the White House. He said there would be dinners there for people who need the food, rather than rich fat cats who have been invited to 1600 Pennsylvania Avenue in the past.

I don't know if Shriver checked this out with McGovern, but it could have raised some very serious logistical problems if the Democratic nominee had been sworn in next January.

Let us assume that McGovern was elected President.

After he's been in the White House a few days, he says to his wife, Eleanor, "We have to give a dinner for the poor people tomorrow night."

"How many will there be?"

"Sarge said one million, three hundred thousand and fifty-four people."

"You've got to be kidding," Eleanor says. "I don't have that many place settings."

"Can't you borrow some from Eunice?"

"Even if I did, we wouldn't have enough room to serve them all."

"Yes, I thought of that. But Sarge promised that the first dinner we had in the White House would be for the poor people, and our credibility is at stake."

"Well, why doesn't *he* give the dinner then? He has more money than we do," Eleanor says angrily.

"Because he's not the President. It doesn't have to be a sit-down dinner, you know. It could be buffet."

"I don't care," Eleanor says, "I'm not going in the kitchen and tell the chef to prepare a buffet for one million, three hundred thousand and fifty-four people."

"Couldn't we have it catered?" McGovern asks.

"This is ridiculous. We'll use up our entire entertainment allowance in our first dinner. What are we going to do for the rest of the four years?"

"Maybe we could freeze the leftovers," McGovern suggests.

"I still say Sarge got into this—let him get out of it," Eleanor says.

"How about the strolling Air Force Strings for entertainment?" McGovern asks.

"You said you were going to cut them out of the defense budget," Eleanor reminds him.

"Oh, yes, I forgot that. Did I promise to cut the Marine Band, too?"

"Down to one French horn and two tuba players."

"Hmm. Maybe Warren Beatty can rustle up the Grateful Dead."

"George, I don't think this is going to work. More than twenty-five million people in this country go to bed hungry every night. You can't just invite one million, three hundred thousand and fifty-four and not expect the others to be very angry."

"Well, you can't have *every* poor person in the country to the White House," McGovern says. "It would be impractical."

"Why didn't you tell that to Shriver before he opened his mouth in West Virginia?"

"Maybe we could have the one million, three hundred thousand and fifty-four for dinner and invite the rest in for coffee and dessert."

"All right," says Eleanor, "I'll do it. But Sarge has to address the invitations."

VI. THE FACTS OF LIFE

THE SOFT SELL

One of the problems with today's economy is that it's very hard to find young people who are good salesmen. Many students coming out of college are more interested in a customer's motivation than they are in closing a sale. They also have a tendency to be too honest, which can play havoc in the retail business.

A friend of mine has a dress shop here in Georgetown, and she told me of the problems she had with a young lady, a psychology major, whom she hired as a salesgirl.

This, in essence, is what happened:

The first day a lady came in the store, and the salesgirl (let us call her Miss Brampton) asked if she could be of help.

"I'd like a suit for the fall," the lady said.

"What price range?" Miss Brampton asked.

"It doesn't make any difference," the lady replied.

"Well, let me ask you this question: Do you want the suit because you need it? Or have you just had a fight with your husband and are trying to get even by making a very expensive purchase?"

"I beg your pardon?" the lady said.

"Perhaps you suspect him of some infidelity, and you think this is the only way you can get back at him."

"I have no idea what you're talking about," the customer said.

"Spending money in anger is a very expensive form of hostility. My advice to you is to think it over for a few days. Try to patch up your differences. Buying a new suit won't save your marriage."

"Thank you very much," the customer said frostily and left the store.

"She's angry with me now," Miss Brampton told the dress shop owner, "but in a week she'll be grateful I talked her out of it."

My friend the shop proprietor decided to let the incident pass; but that afternoon another customer came in, and Miss Brampton asked if she could be of help.

The lady said, "I need something really exciting. I'm going to the Kennedy Center, and I want a dress that will knock everyone dead."

Miss Brampton said, "We have some lovely evening dresses over here for insecure people."

"Insecure people?"

"Oh, yes. Didn't you know that clothes are one of the main ways women compensate for insecurity?"

"I'm not insecure," the lady said angrily.

"Then why do you want to knock them dead at the Kennedy Center? Why can't you be accepted for yourself instead of what you wear? You are a very attractive person, and you have an inner beauty you try to disguise. I can sell you a new dress that will attract attention, but then you would never know if it were you or the dress that made people stop and stare."

By this time the dress shop owner decided to step in.

"Miss Brampton, if the lady wants an evening dress, let her see our evening dresses."

"No," the customer said. "Your girl is right. Why spend five hundred dollars to get a few compliments from people who really don't care what I wear? Thank you for helping me, young lady. It's true I've been insecure all these years and didn't even know it."

The customer walked out of the store.

The final straw for the dress store owner took place an hour later when a coed came in to buy a hotpants outfit, and Miss Brampton gave her thirty minutes on women's lib and then said, "All you do when you buy hotpants is become a sex object."

That night the dress shop owner put a sign in the window: HELP WANTED—NO PSYCHOLOGY MAJORS NEED APPLY.

NOBODY LIKES A SAD BARTENDER

The New York *Times* reported that at Dartmouth's two hundred and first commencement, David Levy of New York City, the highest ranking graduate, gave an address full of despair. Denying he had got anything out of his four years of education, Mr. Levy said, "Take pity on me, those of you who can justify the air you breathe. . . . Send me letters and tell me why life is worth living. Rich parents, write and tell me how money makes your life worthwhile. Dartmouth alumni, tell me how the Dartmouth experience has given value to your life."

He then went on to plead with the graduating class: "And if some one of you out there is also made like me, write me a letter and tell me how you came to appreciate the absurdity of your life."

His remarks were received warmly by his classmates.

In an interview after his speech, Mr. Levy said that he was looking for some menial work until he decided what to do with his life. He said he was considering becoming a bartender "because it's something to do with the hands and it's being with people."

I hadn't planned to write Mr. Levy a letter until I read this last statement:

DEAR DAVE,
Sorry to hear things didn't go too well for you at Dartmouth

and you didn't learn anything. You sounded very depressed in your speech, which of course is your privilege.

My main concern is the revelation that you plan to become a bartender. I don't know how to break this to you, Dave, but nobody likes a depressed person behind the bar.

Most people who go to bars are pretty depressed to start with. The role of the bartender is to cheer them up.

Besides seeing that their glasses are filled, the function of the bartender is to listen to people's troubles and if possible make them forget. The booze plays its role, but the bartender is even more important to the state of people's mental health.

When a fellow comes in and says to the bartender, "The world stinks. Give me a beer," the bartender is supposed to reply, "The world is beautiful. Draft or bottle?"

The customer is depending on the bartender to get him out of his funk. That's why he's paying 50 cents more for beer than he would if he bought it in a store.

Now I know you don't have much use for the profit system, but the guy who owns the bar does, and if you're full of despair, the word is going to get around. "Dalinsky's Bar & Grill has a new bartender, and he sees no reason to justify our existence." Do you know what a rumor like that can do to the sale of Rye and ginger ale?

What I'm trying to tell you, Dave, is that if you're thinking of becoming a bartender, you're going to have to change your thinking on life.

Suppose some guy comes in who has just had a fight with his wife and he's seeking consolation. What do you think he's going to say if you start off the conversation with, "Take pity on me, those of you who can justify the air you breathe"?

You know what he's going to say: "Step outside and I'll punch you right in the nose."

Bartending is not, as you describe it, "menial" work. A good bartender has to be a chemist, a psychologist, a social worker, an economist, and an expert on every facet of life. The right word can send a customer happily home to his loved ones. The wrong word could make him stagger out in the street and lie down in front of a bus.

Dave, before you take this major step, please think about it carefully. It's one thing to believe that life isn't worth living— but it's another thing to bring down the whole neighborhood with you.

Besides, you're never going to make any tips if you keep talking the way you do.

Cheers,
A. B.

THE FACTS OF LIFE

This is the time of the year when fathers sit down and have heart-to-heart talks with their sons.

"Son, now that you have graduated your mothers feels I would not be fulfilling my duties as a father if I did not explain certain facts about life to you."

"Yes, Dad."

"First, I would like to show you a few things that you will have to deal with in the outside world. For example, this item is called a necktie."

"What do you do with it?"

"You tie it around your neck like this and wear it with a shirt."

"What for?"

"Nobody is quite sure. But when you do go out into the cold world, people will expect you to wear one. It's the Establishment's answer to the peace symbol."

"It sure looks funny. What else, Dad?"

"This, my boy, is a suit—what are you laughing at?"

"The jacket matches the pants. Hey, that's really crazy."

"Yes, the jacket does match the pants, and you will be expected to wear them together during the daytime."

"But the pants have a crease in the front. What's that for?"

"I'm not certain of its purpose, but now that you are an adult, you will be expected to keep a crease in your pants."

"Man, what will they think of next?"

"Son, I wish you wouldn't take our talk lightly. Perhaps I should have explained these things to you before, but I didn't want to ruin your school days. Yet what I am telling you now will have a great effect on everything you do."

"Sorry, Dad, but you have to admit wearing a tie and a jacket that matches the pants—what do you call it, a suit?—is a pretty funny idea."

"Can we proceed? These queer-looking leather things are called shoes. Do you have any idea what they're used for?"

"Beats me."

"You put them on your feet to protect them from sharp objects."

"I don't want to wear anything like that, Dad. I'll take my chances."

"I don't know how to break it to you, son, but most places require grown-ups to wear shoes."

"Look, Dad, if you want me to, I will wear a necktie, and I'll even go along with the jacket and matching pants with a crease in them; but I'm not going to put those stupid leather things on my feet."

"Shoes, son, shoes. Believe me, you'll get used to them. After a while you might even get to like them and keep them polished."

"You mean I have to polish them, too?"

"You don't have to, but they look better that way and last longer. Here, put on these socks and then. . . ."

"What are socks?"

"You wear them under the shoes so the leather won't rub your feet."

"I thought the shoes were supposed to protect my feet."

"Provided you wear socks. Son, please don't make this too difficult for me. I'm not very good at explaining the facts of life, but believe me, I've been telling you the truth."

"I'm sorry, Dad, it's just that you've thrown all this stuff at me at one time, and it comes as a shock."

"Perhaps we've talked enough for one day. Tomorrow I'd like to tell you about a thing called a razor."

"Razor? That's a funny word."

FINDING ONESELF

One of the reasons the colleges are suffering from underenrollment is that many high school students are taking a year off "to find themselves."

I was at the Thatchers' home the other night when their son, Rolf, came in and announced that he had decided he would not go to any of the universities that had accepted him because he wanted to spend time bumming around the country.

"Why?" Mr. Thatcher asked.

"Because I have to find myself," Rolf said.

"How can you find yourself any better bumming around the country than going to college?" his father asked him.

"Because it's not happening at school. It's happening out there."

"What's happening out there?" Mrs. Thatcher asked.

"I don't know. That's what I have to find out."

Mr. Thatcher said, "Willy Grugschmid has been on the road for three years now trying to find himself. The only time he knows where he is is when he has to call collect and ask his parents for money."

"It takes some people longer to find themselves than other people," Rolf said defensively.

"Where will you go?" Mrs. Thatcher asked.

"I thought I'd hitchhike to Nevada. Blair Simmons is living on unemployment insurance in Reno. He's with several kids who are trying to find themselves. Then I'll go to Arizona. I know some guys there who are working for Indians making Navajo blankets."

"How do you find yourself making Navajo blankets for the Indians?" Mr. Thatcher wanted to know.

"You work with your hands," Rolf said, "and that gives you time to think."

"Rolf," Mr. Thatcher said, "no one admires your adventurous spirit more than I do. But I have just so much money set aside for your college education. Costs are rising every day. By the time you find yourself I may not be able to send you to college. Couldn't you go to school first and then find yourself later?"

"No," Rolf said. "If I go to school in the fall, I won't be able to concentrate because I'll know I'm missing something out there."

"What, for God's sake?" Mr. Thatcher demanded.

"If I knew, I wouldn't miss it. You see, I have to establish my own identity. If I can't do it in this country, then I plan to go to South America with Edna."

"Edna?" Mrs. Thatcher gasped. "Is Edna trying to find herself, too?"

"Yes. She has a Volkswagen, and she's invited me to go with her."

"How do her parents feel about it?" Mr. Thatcher asked.

"They're pretty mad, but Edna says she has no choice. If she doesn't go, she'll wind up going to school, then getting married and finally she'll become a mother. She sees no future in *that*."

"Suppose she becomes a mother in South America?" Mrs. Thatcher asked.

"It's not going to be that *kind* of trip," Rolf said angrily. "We each have our own sleeping bag."

"It gets cold in the Andes," Mr. Thatcher warned.

"Well, anyway," Rolf said, "I just thought you should know I'm not going to college until I find myself."

"I guess there isn't very much we can do then, is there?" Mr. Thatcher asked. "Will you do us one favor, though? As soon as you find yourself, will you let us know?"

"How will I do that?" Rolf asked.

"Put an ad in the Lost and Found column."

THE DROWNING PLAN

The question of what to do about teen-agers keeps cropping up in every party conversation these days. No matter where you go, parents agree that there is no solution to the problem.

But my friend Drowning has an answer which is at least worth sending up the flagpole.

Drowning told me about his plan the other day.

"I have discovered," he said, "that when I run into people, they tell me that my sixteen-year-old, Ronnie, is one of the sweetest kids they ever met. They say he's polite, loquacious, and intelligent. I can never believe they are talking about my son, who at home is surly, uncommunicative, and a pretty miserable kid all around. At the same time, when I tell them how much I appreciate their children, they all look at me in surprise as if I'm talking about some strangers they have never heard of.

"One day it dawned on me. Everybody thinks the other kid is always better behaved than his own. What makes kids mean and ornery and full of snake venom is living in their own houses with their own parents, whom they consider stupid, narrow-minded, and not worth passing the time of day with.

"Now, since every kid feels this way about his parents and every parent feels this way about his kid, I have come up with the Drowning plan."

"What is it?" I asked excitedly.

"We work out a swap. When a kid announces he can't stand it at home anymore, we swap him with another kid who can't stand it at his home.

"Let me give you an example. Phillip Dutton has had it with his parents. My son, Ronnie, has had it with us. We take Phillip, and they take Ronnie. I like Phillip. He's a nice kid. The Duttons, and God help them, think Ronnie is a jewel. So we take Phil, and they take Ronnie. The swap gives you two peaceful homes."

"Holy smokes," I said. "You may have something."

"Every time we tell our fourteen-year-old daughter, Maria, that she has to be in by twelve o'clock, she cries that Kathy Parrish's daughter, Ellen, doesn't have to be in until one o'clock. Ellen has told my wife the reason she likes our house better than hers is because my wife never makes Maria do the dishes.

"Here we have the perfect swap," Drowning said. "We send Maria to the Parrishes, where she can stay out until one o'clock, and we take Ellen, who will be happy with us because she won't have to do any housework."

"But won't you miss Maria?" I asked.

"If you've seen one teen-age daughter, you've seen them all," Drowning said.

"Besides, since Maria never speaks to us and Ellen does, we

will feel as if we have someone living in our house who is really there.

"The beauty of my plan is that it won't cost anything. We'll make the swap, even-steven, orthodontist work included."

"You could do away with so many power struggles," I said dreamily.

"You better believe it. No one ever hassles with somebody else's kids because they don't give a damn about them. If they don't wash their hair, tough luck for them, and if they don't eat breakfast, it's no skin off the adults' bones. Why yell at someone else's kid when it has nothing to do with you?

"By the same token, the kids have no reason to get sore at people who aren't their parents, because if they're not their parents, what do they have to feel persecuted about?"

"Drowning," I said, "I know you didn't think up your plan to get any personal glory out of it, but I suspect that if it works, you may have a good chance to pick up a Nobel Peace Prize."

COLLEGES NEED YOU

There was a time, not long ago, when parents lived in fear that their children would not be accepted in college. They made the rounds of colleges and universities with their offspring, submitting to countless interviews by hard-faced directors of admissions, who always told them, "Don't get your hopes up."

Well, all this has changed, and most schools are desperate for students to fill their freshman class. Many colleges are now recruiting high school graduates in the same manner they used to recruit high school athletes.

I know a young man who has been applying to colleges this spring, and the response has been phenomenal.

He wrote to one school asking for information and a brochure and received a response in two days: "We are happy to inform you that you have been accepted in the freshman class at Zigzag College. The school term will begin on September 13. Kindly send your deposit of $500 in the enclosed self-addressed envelope."

The young man and his parents thought there was some mistake so they sent off an inquiry to another school, Lieba Tech. A week later a man showed up at the door. He said he was an alumnus of Lieba Tech who lived in Washington and had been asked to come over to speak to the young man about the school.

The alumnus said, "You're just the kind of man Lieba has been looking for."

"But," the boy said, "you don't even know me."

"What is there to know? You're a fine-looking student. I can tell by just looking at you that you would be a credit to the school. Here, just sign the application blank. The school will bill you later."

"I'd like to think about it," the young man said.

"Of course," the alumnus said, "this is a very important decision. Think about it, and I'll call you in a couple of hours."

A week later a man who said he was director of admissions of Sara Lee University showed up at the door. "I just wanted to tell you personally how happy we are to have you as a student at Sara Lee."

"But I haven't applied to Sara Lee," the boy protested.

"We got your name from a spy in the Lieba Tech admissions office. You'd hate Lieba Tech. It has no student parking facilities at all."

"But," the mother said, "isn't Sara Lee a girls' school?"

"If your son agrees to go there, we'll make it coed."

"Do you have a soccer team?" the boy asked.

"You want a soccer team—we'll have a soccer team. You can choose your own uniform."

"I smoke pot," the boy said.

"Who doesn't smoke pot?" the director of admissions asked.

"Don't you even want to look at my school records?"

"School records lie!" the director of admissions yelled. "We want the all-around type of student who is interested in something besides studies."

"I don't know what to say," the boy replied.

Suddenly the director of admissions started to sob. "I don't want to beg, but I have a quota to fill. Give me a break. Come to Sara Lee. My job depends on it. I need you, boy. Why can't you understand that?"

"Please," the father said. "Get off your knees. I assure you we will give Sara Lee our consideration."

As the family led the sobbing director of admissions down the walk to his car, the director asked, "When will I hear from you?"

The boy shook the director's hand and said, "Don't call us—we'll call you."

ZERO POPULATION

The latest news from the Census Bureau is that younger women are refusing to have children, and the United States is fast approaching a "zero population growth" rate. This means the death rate and birthrate figures in the country will soon be even.

Disturbed by this information, I sought out three young ladies in a coffeehouse to find out what had gone wrong. Their names were Fern, Clara, and Mary Jane, and they were sitting with three boys—Harry, Fred, and Claude.

"Ladies," I said, "I have just read in the newspapers that women in this country only had an average of 2.4 children in 1971 as opposed to 2.9 children in 1967, and if the trend continues, they will be down to 2.1 in a few years, which could mean zero population growth. How can you explain it?"

"Who wants kids?" Fern asked.

"But," I said, "that is the role of women—to reproduce their own kind."

"That's the point," Clara said. "Who wants to reproduce people like us?"

"I don't understand," I said.

Clara said, "It's a generation problem. Your generation had a high opinion of yourselves. You thought you were wonderful people—brave, strong, honest, law-abiding, productive, and God-fearing. Therefore, you wanted to reproduce more of the same.

"You assumed that your offspring would be just like you, and you wanted to flood the country with little copies of yourself.

"Well, it didn't work out that way," Clara concluded. "You produced an entirely different breed, and we've decided we don't want any more like us because we can't stand each other."

"Why should we make babies who are as unhappy and miserable as we are?" Mary Jane asked.

"I don't want any kids like Harry," Fern said.

"But," Harry protested, "you're my girlfriend."

"I don't mind you as my boyfriend," Fern said, "but I couldn't stand you as my son."

"It's true. I could never think of raising a Claude or a Fred. I wouldn't have the stomach for it."

"That isn't a nice thing to say," Fred said defensively.

"Well," Clara replied, "would you like to be the father of Fern or Mary Jane or Harry or Claude?"

"I wouldn't even want to be the father of me," Fred said.

"If I understand you," I said, "the reason why you don't want to have babies is that you're afraid they'll all turn out like you."

"You got it, Pops," Fern said. "We know what we've done to our parents, and we're not about to let our kids do that to us."

Clara said, "I couldn't hassle with my kids the way I hassle with my mother. I'd go up the wall."

"But," I protested, "if all of you feel that way, the American people—the greatest, most magnificent and wondrous people the world has ever seen—could go down the drain."

"It's not our fault," Mary Jane said. "We're physically but not mentally equipped for it."

Fern said, "Once the country gets down to zero population growth, I might reconsider the whole proposition. But at the moment, I'd rather take the money it costs to raise a child and go to Europe."

"Even buying a Honda motorcycle," Harry said, "would be more fun than having a kid like me."

COMMENCEMENT 1973

It's time for those enlightening, inspiring commencement speeches again. Most students are willing to sit through them just so they can get their diplomas. What isn't known is that what commencement speakers are saying and what they're thinking are quite different:

"My fellow graduates,

"It is indeed a great pleasure for me to be here on what is probably the most important day of your lives."

(If it weren't for this damn honorary degree, I could have been playing golf this afternoon.)

"I know these are troubled times for all of us. I am troubled; you are troubled; we are troubled; they are troubled. Everyone is troubled."

(I wish they wouldn't sit the coeds in the first row with their legs sticking out of their gowns. It's hard to concentrate.)

"The problem is not that we are troubled, but what we can do about it. Certainly you can throw your hands in the air and say, 'It's hopeless.' Or you can say, 'Give us your troubles and let us solve them for you.' "

(I wonder if any of the wire services will ask for copies of my speech.)

"I would be the first one to admit that our generation has not succeeded in conquering the great issues of the day—pollution, poverty, racism, war, and hunger."

(At least they know I've got humility.)

"But we have started the fight. You must pick up the weapons that we have left on the battlefield and continue the struggle. The journey of a thousand miles begins with one step."

(Is it possible that the blonde sitting in the end seat just winked at me? Why, I'm old enough to be her father. But then again, she might be a graduate student.)

"We are different from all of God's other creatures in that we can do something about our environment. We can harness the sun's energy; we can control our waters with concrete; we can enrich the earth with chemicals."

(It could be my imagination, but half those graduates out there look stoned.)

"But man also has the capacity to wreak havoc on the earth. And I might add, with a bow toward women's lib, that woman has this capacity as well."

(I thought that would get a laugh. These kids don't have any sense of humor at all.)

"Each man must decide for himself or herself what path he or she will take. Will he or she pay homage to the sun, or will he or she crawl into a cave and curse the darkness?"

(I'll bet no one has ever heard it put that way before.)

"I would be a fool to say that your diploma is a ticket to a better life. It is not what you hold in your hand, but what you hold in your head and your heart that will decide your destiny."

(By God, she winked at me again. And now she's smiling. Maybe she needs a job. I wonder if she takes shorthand?)

"Today is the first day of the rest of your life. Your parents and teachers have done all they can for you. It is now up to every one of you to carry the ball.

"We can't all get to the Super Bowl, but we can all play the game. We can't all win the World Series, but we can still swing at the ball. The important thing is not to be a spectator in the stands, but to go out on the field and fight for what you believe in."

(I wonder if *Time* magazine will pick that up?)

"So, in conclusion, I wish to say that if I had the choice of any time in history to live, I would choose now. And if I had any choice of graduating, I would prefer to graduate in the class of 1973. To quote an old song, 'Pack up your troubles in your old kit bag and smile, smile, smile.' Thank you."

(That's not much of an ovation. Maybe I didn't read it well.)

VII. WE'RE NUMBER ONE

FATHER'S DAY

DEAR DAD,

Just wanted to wish you a happy Father's Day. Been thinking a lot about you lately. Did you send the money order in care of American Express in Madrid or in care of American Express in Barcelona? American Express here in Madrid says they never received it, so you better raise hell with them because they're being very loose with your money.

I'm pulling out from Madrid for the Costa del Sol and then will probably go over to Morocco. There's an American Express in Casablanca, and a friend told me they're really good on receiving money orders. Hope you're not working too hard. I'll wait here two more days, just in case the money order comes through. I'm real sorry I can't be with you on Father's Day, but I didn't want to let it pass without saying hello.

Love,
GEORGE

DEAR DAD,

I'm taking the opportunity of Father's Day to tell you something important. I've decided you were right—there's more to life than having a good time bumming around and not caring about the world.

I've decided my attitude has been selfish and unrealistic and hasn't helped me or you. I know you warned me that I would come to this realization, but I had to find it out myself. And so, Dad, next week, on my forty-seventh birthday, I'm going to go out and look for a job.

Sincerely,
EDWARD

DEAR POP,

With Father's Day coming up on Sunday, I thought I ought to get a short note off to you and tell you I think you're the best daddy in the whole world. Also, I think I'm pregnant.

But don't get excited. Tommy said he'd marry me when he gets out of law school, which should be in three years.

I hope you have a wonderful and relaxed Father's Day.

Love,
INGER

DEAR DAD,

I don't know how to say this to you. It's probably the hardest letter I've ever had to write, and coming just before Father's Day doesn't make it any easier.

You always taught me to think for myself and make my own decisions. I remember when I visited you at the factory last year, you said, "Son, in business you have to live your own life. Don't let personal things influence your decisions."

Well, Dad, I've been thinking a lot since then about what you said, and this is what I have to tell you. My conglomerate bought out your company last week, and you're fired.

Love,
FRED

DEAR FATHER,

Your son Gerald bought a red and blue tie from us for Father's Day, and we'd like to inform you that we have several suits on sale that go with it. Why not visit our fitting rooms and get the right suit to go with the tie? A lot of thought went into your son's gift, and you owe it to him to buy a suit to complement the tie he gave you.

Yours truly,
ABELARD AND THOMAS
Men's Clothiers, Est. 1894

P.S. We are open on Father's Day until midnight.

THE GREAT $100-A-POUND BET

We were sitting in the Sans Souci Restaurant in Washington on a hot August afternoon. Edward Bennett Williams, the famous defense lawyer, and I had each just finished off a mousse chocolate, and as we sipped our coffee, we discussed different reasons why we couldn't lose weight.

"We need an incentive," I said. "Something that is bigger than both of us."

"I know an incentive," Williams said, eating a petit four.

"What is it?" I asked, nibbling on a sugar-coated strawberry.

"Greed," Williams replied. "Greed has been the motivating force in both our lives."

I couldn't argue with that.

"We will make a bet as to who can lose the most weight in a certain amount of time at a hundred dollars a pound."

"Jeez," I said. "You mean if I lose twenty-five pounds and you only lose fifteen, you have to pay me a thousand dollars?"

"Or," said Williams, "if I lose twenty and you only lose five, you have to pay me fifteen hundred dollars."

We agreed on the rules. We would proceed to the Metropolitan Club in Washington after lunch (Williams is a member), weigh in at the Health Club. Then we would weigh in three months later, the day before Thanksgiving at exactly noon. Arnie, the head of the Health Club, would keep our starting weights in a locked safe.

After lunch, we went to the Health Club, stripped to the buff, and weighed in. Williams tipped the scales at exactly 220 pounds. I weighed in at exactly 190 pounds and the battle was on.

My strategy was to tell everyone about the bet in hopes they would give me the moral strength to win it. Several people who knew Williams' predilection for cocktails and desserts asked for a piece of my action. Not only were they certain Williams would be unable to lose the weight, but they pointed out that since he was also the president of the Washington Redskins football team, and with the bet taking place at the height of the football season, Williams would soon be eating a pound of French bread a day.

We both used psychological warfare tactics. One noontime I sent a tray of French pastries to Williams' office when he'd decided not to go to lunch. Two evenings later a large chocolate layer cake was delivered to my home with a note, "Always thinking of you—Eddie."

I sent Williams a book on ice cream. He gave me a $15 gift certificate for Fanny Farmer Candies. Both our secretaries were getting fat.

Since everyone knew about the bet, I kept getting intelligence reports every day. Williams, who was defending Louis Wolfson in a case being tried in New York City, was seen at Luchow's eating six potato pancakes. A week later, he was reported to have been spotted at P. J. Clarke's at three o'clock in the morning, surrounded by nothing but fried onion rings.

In the meantime, I worked desperately to lose some weight. Since I don't drink liquor, every pound I took off was painful.

In six weeks, I had taken off ten pounds. Williams, by his own admission, had put on six.

He demanded a summit conference at Paul Young's Restaurant.

"I want to call off the bet," he said. "I didn't realize I would have to try the Wolfson case in New York, as well as deal with the Redskins. I can't take off weight under pressure."

"No chance of calling off the bet," I said.

"But I'm sixteen hundred dollars behind," he protested.

"I'll tell you what I'll do," I said. "If you lose, you have to give the money to the United Jewish Appeal. If I lose, I'll give it to your favorite charity. This way we won't be taking money from each other. What do you want me to give it to?"

"Cardinal O'Boyle's Right to Live Committee," said Williams. "It's an anti-abortion organization that helps pregnant girls."

A few weeks later, at Duke Zeibert's Restaurant, the Israeli Ambassador Yitzhak Rabin passed by our table, and I introduced Williams to him. "Mr. Ambassador," I said, "Mr. Williams is going to buy Israel a new jet fighter plane and I think you should thank him personally."

The ambassador said he was very happy Williams cared that much about Israel.

Williams muttered something inaudible. After the ambassador left, Williams said, "Now you've done it. You have humiliated me in front of the Israeli ambassador. You have gotten me mad. I am going to get you if it's the last thing I do." Then he ordered another scotch and soda.

The day before Thanksgiving was bright and clear. The night before I had taken a dose of milk of magnesia (Williams, I heard later, had taken dehydration pills). I went to the YMCA and worked out for an hour and then spent another hour in the steam room. In three months I had managed to take off 16 pounds. I was certain this was enough. As a matter of fact, I was so sure of myself that I had hired a violinist for $50 to play for the weighing in. I had also organized a large victory luncheon for reporters at the Sans Souci to follow the weigh-in.

We could have sold $10,000 worth of tickets to the weighing in. All of Washington knew about the bet, and several women, including Ethel Kennedy, offered to hold our clothes.

But Williams was in a foul mood, and he called me and said, "I'll pay you the money, but if anyone shows up in the locker room for the weigh-in, the bet is off."

I arrived at the Metropolitan Health Club at ten of twelve. Arnie told me Williams was in the steam room, where he had been since ten. I went into the steam room, but he refused to shake my hand. "Let's go," he said.

"I'd like to take off another pound, if it's all the same to you," I said.

"You trying to forfeit the match?" he asked.

I followed him out of the steam room. "What a terrible loser," I said.

We both walked into the locker room where the scale was. I opened the door to the shower, and out stepped my violinist playing "Hearts and Flowers." Williams was in a rage.

"No one said anything about music at the weigh-in," he protested.

"You didn't say anything about *not* having music," I replied.

As I got on the scale, the violinist played "Let a Winner Lead the Way." I weighed in at exactly 174 pounds.

Williams then got on the scale. I couldn't believe it. He was down from 220 to 199 pounds. I demanded a recount. The scale still showed 199. I had lost $500. The fickle violinist immediately broke into "Hail to the Redskins."

It was one of the great upsets in diet history. Williams had lost twenty-one pounds in two weeks, probably nineteen of it in water.

My victory luncheon at the Sans Souci turned into a bitter meal of humiliation and abuse. The reporters asked me if I would have done anything differently, and I replied, "As I look back on it, my big mistake, besides peaking too early, was introducing the Israeli ambassador to Williams at Duke Zeibert's."

Now the only thing I have to show for my painful three months is a thank-you letter from Cardinal O'Boyle telling me how happy I made all the unmarried Catholic girls in Washington.

CLEAN YOUR ROOM

You don't really feel the generation gap in this country until a son or daughter comes home from college for Christmas. Then it strikes you how out of it you really are.

This dialogue probably took place all over America last Christmas week:

"Nancy, you've been home from school for three days now. Why don't you clean up your room?"

"We don't have to clean up our rooms at college, Mother."

"That's very nice, Nancy, and I'm happy you're going to such a freewheeling institution. But while you're in the house, your father and I would like you to clean up your room."

"What difference does it make? It's *my* room."

"I know, dear, and it really doesn't mean that much to me. But your father has a great fear of the plague. He said this morning if it is going to start anywhere in this country, it's going to start in your room."

"Mother, you people aren't interested in anything that's relevant. Do you realize how the major corporations are polluting our environment?"

"Your father and I are very worried about it. But right now we're more concerned with the pollution in your bedroom. You haven't made your bed since you came home."

"I never make it up at the dorm."

"Of course you don't, and I'm sure the time you save goes toward your education. But we still have these old-fashioned ideas about making beds in the morning, and we can't shake them. Since you're home for such a short time, why don't you do it to humor us?"

"For heaven's sake, Mother, I'm grown up now. Why do you have to treat me like a child?"

"We're not treating you like a child. But it's very hard for us to realize you're an adult when you throw all your clothes on the floor."

"I haven't thrown all my clothes on the floor. Those are just the clothes I wore yesterday."

"Forgive me. I exaggerated. Well, how about the dirty dishes and empty soft-drink cans on your desk? Are you collecting them for a science project?"

"Mother, you don't understand us. You people were brought up to have clean rooms. But our generation doesn't care about things like that. It's what you have in your head that counts."

"No one respects education more than your father and I do, particularly at the prices they're charging. But we can't see how living in squalor can improve your mind."

"That's because of your priorities. You would rather have me make up my bed and pick up my clothes than become a free spirit who thinks for myself."

"We're not trying to stifle your free spirit. It's just that our

Blue Cross has run out, and we have no protection in case anybody in the family catches typhoid."

"All right, I'll clean up my room if it means that much to you. But I want you to know you've ruined my vacation."

"It was a calculated risk I had to take. Oh, by the way, I know this is a terrible thing to ask of you, but would you mind helping me wash the dinner dishes?"

"Wash dishes? Nobody washes dishes at school."

"Your father and I were afraid of that."

A MARRIAGE CONTRACT

The chief steward of the *Christina*, Aristotle Onassis' yacht, has written a book in which he says that Mr. Onassis and his wife, the former Jacqueline Kennedy, signed a marriage contract with 170 clauses in it.

According to the steward, Christian Kafarakis, the contract stipulates separate bedrooms for the couple, lays down the rules as to how much time the couple must spend together, and spells out financial arrangements. These include a $600,000 yearly allowance for Mrs. Onassis, in addition to any gifts Mr. Onassis might give her, as well as a provision that if Mr. Onassis ever leaves his wife, Mrs. Onassis will receive the sum of $9,600,000 for every year of their marriage.

If Mrs. Onassis were to leave Mr. Onassis, she would receive a lump sum of $18,000,000 under the terms of the alleged contract. Mr. Onassis also is said to have provided $100,000,000 in his will—for Mrs. Onassis.

A spokeswoman for Mrs. Onassis categorically and unequivocally denied that such a marriage contract exists and called the story nonsense.

I have no knowledge of whether such a contract does exist and shall leave Mr. Onassis and his ex-steward to fight that one out.

But I do know that marriage contracts, particularly in Europe, are not uncommon, and as a matter of fact, since both my wife and I were living in Paris when we wanted to get married, we signed one.

Our marriage contract, which has 169 clauses in it, was thrashed out over a period of months before the wedding was agreed to.

It provides for the following, among other things:

—I have to spend half the year with my wife (she tried to hold out for seven months). This time can be broken up any way I want it. I am permitted to go on lectures, attend openings of Hilton Hotels, go to pro football games, and attend homecoming weekends. For every day less than six months that I don't spend with her, I have to give her $2.50 or its equivalent in trading stamps.

—I am committed under the terms of the contract to give my wife $600 a year for her pleasure, safety, clothes, hairdresser, cosmetics, and the care of the house. The $600 does not include gasoline for the car, provided she uses it on family business.

—If I want to leave my wife, I must give her the sum of $50 for every year we have been married.

—If she wants to leave me, she will receive a flat settlement of $185.50.

—As long as we are living together, I must provide my wife with detergents, mops, plastic garbage bags, and a lawn mower.

—I also am obligated to pay for the veterinarian in case we have a dog.

—While we are married, my wife has custody of the children all day and most evenings. For this she is given the extra sum of $10 a week.

—If we have a fight, I must be the one to sleep on the couch in the living room.

—I must also give her the sum of $5 if I pay too much attention to another girl at a party.

These are more or less the financial details of our marriage contract, and the only reason I'm revealing them at this time is that our cleaning woman just quit, and I understand she's going to sell the terms to the *National Enquirer*. It would embarrass my wife something terrible if the marriage agreement ever became public.

A CURE FOR THE COMMON COLD

A new cure for the "common cold" couldn't have come too soon. Recently two Israeli researchers announced they had been able to cure nose colds by chilling the big toes of patients' feet. The Israelis claimed that the sudden temporary chilling of the big toes almost immediately brings about a lowering of the normal temperature within the nose. And lowering the nasal temperature dries up the nostrils, thereby curing the cold.

At the time the story appeared on the front pages of newspapers and on television I was in bed with a severe nose cold, and my wife said to me, "Let's try it. What have you got to lose?"

The Israeli researchers said they had developed a special indirect cooling apparatus adapted to the shape of the big toe. It uses a refrigerant chemical called dichloro difluoromethane, which can chill a toe in less than a minute. Since we didn't have this chemical available, my wife decided to tape an ice cube on each toe.

I lay there with my feet sticking out of each side of the bed and ice cubes on my big toes.

"How do you feel?" she asked.

"About the same."

"Then why are you laughing?"

"The water trickling between my toes makes me ticklish."

The ice cubes kept melting, and I kept sneezing and giggling, so my wife said, "Maybe ice cubes aren't the answer. Would you consider putting both your feet in the refrigerator?"

"You have to be kidding," I said.

"You have everything to gain," she said, taking the ice cubes off my toes and handing me a bathrobe.

I sat on a kitchen chair while she removed the food from the shelves of the refrigerator. "We'll try it in this part of the fridge, and if it doesn't work, we'll put your feet in the deepfreeze."

"I'd just as soon drink plenty of liquids and take aspirin."

"There," she said, "put your feet on the third shelf and read a book."

Five minutes later she said, "Do you feel anything?"

"Nothing at all," I said.

"Then your cold is gone?"

"No, my toes are frozen. I can't move them."

"They are sort of blue. Maybe you better take them out."

"Where should I put them, in the oven?"

"There has to be some way of freezing your toes without giving you frostbite," my wife said.

"Maybe I could put them in the mashed potatoes of a frozen TV dinner?"

"Perhaps," she said, "if you stuck your feet against the air-conditioning vent."

"I'd rather put them out the window."

"I know, I'll make two frozen daiquiris, and you can put a big toe in each one. That way they'll freeze, but you won't suffer."

She made two double daiquiris (banana) and inserted a toe in each glass. I relaxed as nature took its course. My body temperature slowly went down, and in half an hour my cold was gone. Now if I can just get rid of this hangover.

THE BAD BACK PROBLEM

The biggest problem this country faces is not the economy, law 'n' order, the war, or revolution, but bad backs.

It turns out that everyone in this country has back trouble, and until a cure is found for it, we will never be able to solve our other difficulties.

I discovered this recently when my wife's back went out on her while she was playing tennis. I immediately sent her off to an orthopedic surgeon, who told her she had a ruptured disc and would have to go in traction and wear a sponge collar around her neck.

It was her collar that gave us the tipoff on how many bad backs there are in this country. People rarely talk about their backs until they see someone else wearing a collar. Then they open up and confess about their own bad back troubles.

The first time I took my wife to a party with her collar around her neck a friend said, "What are you doing about it?"

My wife said she was going to an orthopedic doctor.

"They don't know anything," the friend said. "What you need for a bad back is a neurosurgeon."

The next day we located one of the best neurosurgeons in the country. After careful examination, he concluded my wife had a ruptured disc and needed traction and advised her to wear a sponge collar around her neck.

Since this was the same diagnosis she got from the orthopedic man, my wife was naturally disappointed.

But a few days later her spirits picked up. She told me when I got home, "The man who rakes our leaves said that neurosurgeons don't know anything about backs. He said the best way to get rid of my bad back was to sleep on the floor."

"Well, the guy who rakes leaves should know," I said.

A week later she called me at the office. "Anabelle knows a woman in Seven Corners who can cure crooked spines with her fingernails. She has never worked on someone who didn't get better."

Three days later my wife got wind of an acupuncturist who lived in Chinatown. Her friend Aggie said, "Four gold needles and you'll be playing tennis in a week."

Before she could look up the acupuncture doctor, her sister called from Cincinnati and told her the only way to get rid of her bad back was through yoga and meditation.

Several weeks went by, and while my wife did continue her traction, her heart wasn't in it.

"It seems so slow," she protested to me. "The hairdresser knows a spa in Italy that specializes in mud baths for bad backs."

"If it doesn't work, you can always go to Lourdes," I said.

But while she was getting her passport for Italy, a brother-in-law from West Virginia called in to tell about a new miracle cure for backs that some lady in the Blue Ridge Mountains had developed from herbs.

"It sounds better than mud baths," I said.

The ointment arrived, and surprisingly, it had no effect on my wife's back.

Having tried everything, we decided to go back to the neurosurgeon on the off chance that he might know something about her problem that the hairdresser didn't.

The doctor said she was doing fine but would have to stay in traction for another month.

You can imagine her depressed state of mind when she left the office. But fortunately, on the way home the cabdriver recognized her symptoms and said, "I know a hypnotist in Alexandria who specializes in nothing but ruptured discs."

CHRISTMAS CARDS TELL ALL

Christmas cards reveal a great deal more about America than one would like to admit. They show as well as anything what a restless society we've become.

The other day my wife was opening cards, and she was puzzled by one from Hal and Virginia Lark.

"I thought Hal's wife's name was Frieda," she said.

"So did I. Maybe she changed it to Virginia," I suggested.

The next day the mystery was cleared up when we received a Christmas card from the McDowalls.

"We don't know any McDowalls," my wife said.

"We must, or they wouldn't have sent us a Christmas card."

"The handwriting looks familiar," my wife said. "As a matter of fact, it looks exactly like Frieda Lark's signature."

"How could it be Frieda's Lark's signature if it was sent by the McDowalls?"

"Maybe Frieda is no longer a Lark!" my wife exclaimed.

"Then that means Hal married a girl named Virginia, and Frieda married a guy named McDowall."

"I wish people would tell me these things before I sent out *my* Christmas cards."

She opened a few other cards and then came to one which she studied carefully. "This photograph is very peculiar. I could swear it was Myrna Tuttle, but the card says it's from the Lindstroms."

I looked at it. "It sure does seem to be Myrna. Wait a minute. Aren't those Myrna's twins on the sailboat?"

"Yes," my wife said. "But I don't recognize the man at the wheel."

"That's probably Lindstrom," I said.

"I wonder what happened to Dick Tuttle?"

"Look through your cards. The answer is probably there."

My wife went through the cards. "You're right. Here's one from the Tuttles. It's Dick Tuttle, all right, but I don't recognize the woman or the children sitting on the lawn."

"They're probably *her* children," I said.

"Well, at least that takes care of the Tuttle problem," she said.

The next day, when I came home from work, my wife was waiting for me with more cards.

"Helen Coates is now Helen Samovar, Marty Keeler has a new wife named Zelda, and we got separate Christmas cards from Lars and Margie Payne. His came from San Francisco, and hers came from Fort Lauderdale."

"I got a few at the office," I said. "Apparently Bob Elmendorf got custody of the five children because his card shows him sitting on a fence with a new wife and eight kids."

"Who are the other three?" my wife wanted to know.

"*Her* kids. I wonder why Lucy Elmendorf didn't get custody of the children?"

"This card," my wife said, "may explain it. It's from Lucy, and she says she's living in Guadeloupe with a fantastic penniless young artist whom she met when she went to visit her sister in Los Angeles.

"We also got a card from the Madisons," she added. "They still seem to be together."

"Forget it," I said. "I just received a wire at the office from Bill Madison. It says DISREGARD CHRISTMAS GREETINGS. LETTER FOLLOWS."

MARRIAGE AND THE GROSS NATIONAL PRODUCT

For the first time, it has been conclusively proved that the

United States loses 34,000,000 man-hours of work each week owing to fights between husbands and wives.

Professor Heinrich Applebaum of the Institute for Advanced Marital Development has just completed a study on marriage disputes and their effect on the gross national product.

"My study," Professor Applebaum told me, "indicates that production is affected even more by domestic fights than alcoholism."

"How can that be?"

"For some reason, which we still have not been able to determine, the American wife prefers to start all fights with her husband at bedtime. These fights, which last on the average of two or three hours, prevent the man from getting any sleep. The next day he is completely useless at his job, causing accidents, grave errors in bookkeeping, and making horrible decisions in a groggy state of mind."

"That's serious," I admitted.

"We suspected it all along," Applebaum said. "But now we have the data to back it up. This is a case history of a typical American couple in Detroit whom we followed through from dinnertime one evening to lunch the next day:

"Saxby came home at six P.M., had a dry martini, watched the evening news, and then shared a delicious dinner with his wife and three children. After dinner he took a bath, read the evening paper and watched the *Dean Martin Show*. The wife did the dishes, called her mother, took her bath, and read a chapter of *The Godfather*.

"Mr. Saxby said, 'Good night, dear. I have an early meeting tomorrow with some subcontractors to discuss a very important matter.'

"Mrs. Saxby said, 'Good night, dear.'

"Five minutes later Mrs. Saxby asked, 'Why don't you ever talk to me?'

"Saxby, who was just dozing off, responded, 'Huh?'

" 'You never talk to me anymore. You have an awful lot to say to your friends, but you don't have anything to say to me.'

" 'I talk to you,' Saxby said, getting a good grip on his pillow. 'We talk all the time.'

" 'But you never say anything. You don't talk to your

children either. As far as we're concerned, you're just a boarder here.'

"Saxby rolled over on his stomach. 'You're right, I should talk more to all of you. Good night, dear.'

" 'That's typical of you,' Mrs. Saxby said, lighting a cigarette. 'You think you can just end a discussion by saying I'm right. It doesn't wash anymore. You won't even talk to me now.'

" 'I'd love to talk to you,' Saxby said, 'but it's midnight, and I have this meeting with the subcontractors tomorrow.'

" 'Of course. Your work is so much more important than your home life. Why don't you just move into the office and forget about us?'

"Saxby started punching the pillow. 'Look, I tell you what. Why don't I come home early from work tomorrow and we'll discuss it then?'

" 'I want to discuss it now. Tomorrow it might not bother me.' "

The case history said the Saxbys stayed awake until three o'clock in the morning discussing not only why Saxby didn't talk to his wife but also an old girlfriend that Saxby had before he was married, a questionable joke Saxby had told at a dinner party the previous week, a poker game Saxby had gone to a year ago, and the fact that he had missed his seventeen-year-old daughter's birthday party when she was three years old.

The next morning, according to the case history, Saxby was so sleepy he made a mistake on the subcontracting job, and three months later the Ford Motor Company had to recall 1,000,000 cars.

WE'RE NUMBER ONE

The subject of sex in marriage is no longer taboo, and more and more institutes have been set up to help married couples find sexual happiness together.

Dr. Henrico Belladonna, who runs the Clinic of Marital Bliss in Spring Valley, told me, "One of the big discoveries we psychologists have made is that not all sexual problems in today's marriages can be attributed to fear. Our studies indicate that fear now ranks only second as a reason for sexual hang-ups."

"What is number one?" I asked.

"I'll show you," he said. "I have a couple coming in now. Why don't you go over and sit in that chair and observe what happens?"

A man and wife entered nervously, and the doctor asked them to be seated.

Dr. Belladonna waited for them to say something. Finally the husband spoke up. "Doctor, we've come to your institute as a last resort. Our sex life seems to be on the rocks, and we don't know what to do about it."

Dr. Belladonna said, "I would like to ask you a few questions. How often do you have relations each week?"

"Never," the wife said.

"Never?" Dr. Belladonna asked.

"It isn't that we don't want to," the husband said. "It's just that we don't seem to have the time anymore."

"I see," said Dr. Belladonna. "Well, let's look into that. What's wrong with Monday night?"

"Oh," said the husband, "we can't do it on Mondays. That's the *ABC Football Game of the Week*. It's never over until midnight."

"You prefer watching football to making love?" Dr. Belladonna asked.

"That's a stupid question," the husband said angrily. "Doesn't everybody?"

"Not *everybody*," Dr. Belladonna said. "Don't you find it strange that you prefer Howard Cosell to your own wife?"

"Are you trying to say I have homosexual tendencies?" the husband yelled.

"I didn't say that at all," Dr. Belladonna replied. "But it is true you'd rather watch twenty-two men knock each other down for three hours than make love to your wife."

"You're twisting things around," the husband said. "I can make love to my wife anytime, but how often can I see a good football game?"

"All right, let's forget about Mondays," Dr. Belladonna said. "What about Tuesday night?"

"There's basketball to watch on Tuesday night. You want me to give up basketball, too?"

"I don't want you to give up anything. What about Wednesday nights?"

"He has hockey on Wednesday nights," the wife said.

"And Thursdays? Do you have anything to watch on Thursday nights?" Dr. Belladonna asked.

"No," said the husband. "But I'm pretty tired from staying up late on Monday, Tuesday, and Wednesday nights. A guy has to rest *sometime*."

"Fridays?" Dr. Belladonna asked.

"Friday is another basketball night," the husband said. "And Saturday night I like to get to bed early so I can watch the TV football games on Sunday afternoon."

"Well," said Dr. Belladonna, "that seems to take care of the week."

"Can you help us, Doctor?" the wife asked.

"It means a lot to us," the husband said. "We're willing to do anything to find happiness together."

Dr. Belladonna asked, "What are you doing for the rest of the afternoon?"

The husband looked at his *TV Guide*. "This afternoon's no good. I have a golf game to watch at four."

VIII. WORKING ON THE RAILROAD

A PRAYER FOR TOURISTS

According to the *Times* of London, the Greek Orthodox Church issued a new prayer asking the Lord to protect the Greek people from tourists. The prayer, which is to be said by monks and nuns every morning and every evening, goes like this:

"Lord Jesus Christ, Son of God, have mercy on the cities, the islands, and the villages of our Orthodox fatherland, as well as the holy monasteries, which are scourged by the worldly touristic wave.

"Grace us with a solution to this dramatic problem and protect our brethren who are sorely tried by the modernistic spirit of these contemporary Western invaders."

Now it's only fair if the monks and nuns are beseeching the Lord with antitourist prayers that the tourists get equal time. So I have written a prayer for tourists which they must recite when they get up in the morning and go to bed at night.

It goes like this:

"Heavenly Father, look down on us your humble obedient tourist servants who are doomed to travel this earth, taking photographs, mailing postcards, buying souvenirs, and walking about in drip-dry underwear.

"We beseech you, O Lord, to see that our plane is not hijacked, our luggage is not lost, and our overweight baggage goes unnoticed.

"Protect us from surly and unscrupulous taxi drivers, avaricious porters, and unlicensed English-speaking guides.

"Give us this day divine guidance in the selection of our hotels that we may find our reservations honored, our rooms made up, and hot water running from the faucets (if it is at all possible).

"We pray that the telephones work and that the operators speak our tongue and that there is no mail waiting from our children which would force us to cancel the rest of our trip.

"Lead us, dear Lord, to good inexpensive restaurants where the food is superb, the waiters friendly, and the wine included in the price of the meal.

"Give us the wisdom to tip correctly in currencies we do not understand. Forgive us for undertipping out of ignorance and overtipping out of fear. Make the natives love us for what we are and not for what we can contribute to their worldly goods.

"Grant us the strength to visit the museums, the cathedrals, the palaces, and the castles listed as 'musts' in the guidebooks.

"And if perchance we skip a historic monument to take a nap after lunch, have mercy on us, for our flesh is weak."

(This part of the prayer is for husbands.)

"Dear God, keep our wives from shopping sprees and protect them from 'bargains' they don't need or can't afford. Lead them not into temptation, for they know not what they do."

(This part of the prayer is for wives.)

"Almighty Father, keep our husbands from looking at foreign women and comparing them to us.

"Save them from making fools of themselves in cafés and nightclubs. Above all, please do not forgive them their trespasses, for they know exactly what they do."

(Together.) "And when our voyage is over, and we return to our loved ones, grant us the favor of finding someone who will look at our home movies and listen to our stories, so our lives as tourists will not have been in vain.

"This we ask you in the Name of Conrad Hilton, Thomas Cook, and the American Express. Amen."

THE $200 UNDERSTANDING

The $200 student round-trip air fare to Europe caused a sensation in travel circles. What started out as a very gloomy time for the airlines may have turned out to be the most exciting summer the aviation business has had in years.

It isn't generally known how the $200 fare came about. Originally the scheduled airlines charged a young person more than $450 to fly round trip from New York to London or Paris.

With the economy in the doldrums this was too much for most parents to afford.

Finally, as summer approached, a meeting was arranged in New York between the major airline companies and a representative group of parents.

It opened with some rancor. A parent said, "The airlines are taking advantage of a hopeless situation. They know they have us in a bind. We can't afford to spend four hundred and fifty dollars to send our kids to Europe, and at the same time, if we keep them at home this summer, we'll all go nuts."

An airline executive defended the high fares. "The reason we have to charge so much is that we find fewer and fewer parents are going abroad. If we can't make a profit on volume, we have to make it on a high markup."

"You know very well why we can't go abroad," a father said. "How can we take a vacation and leave our teen-agers at home? We can't even go away for a weekend without the roof falling in."

A second parent said, "The airlines owe it to us to get our children out of our hair."

"But," an airline executive protested, "we are having severe financial difficulties as it is. We cannot afford to reduce fares."

"Perhaps," interjected another official "we might see our way clear to give young people a ten percent reduction."

"I put it to you," a father said. "If we can't send our kids to Europe, then we can't go on our own, and if we can't go, you're going to be flying empty 747's for the next five years. You figure out a way of getting the kids out of the house, and then we'll start talking to you about going to Europe ourselves."

The airline executives asked for a two-hour adjournment. They came back and said, "This is our final offer. We will give your children a thirty percent discount on round-trip fares to Europe on a standby basis."

"It won't wash," a parent said angrily. "If they're on a standby basis, we have no assurance they'll get on the plane. When we take them to the airport, we don't want to see them again until September."

"That's right," a mother said. "We've had them all year. Let Europe worry about them for a while."

The executives asked for another adjournment. Then, when the meeting recommenced, a spokesman said, "We have consulted with our sales department, and while it will be a great sacrifice, we think we can fly your children to Europe and back for around two hundred dollars."

"It's about time," one of the parents said.

"Then you accept?" the spokesman said.

"I don't believe there is a parent in America who wouldn't spend two hundred dollars to get rid of a teen-ager," a mother said.

"Gentlemen," a father added, "by making it possible for our children to go abroad this summer, you have not only saved the airlines, you have also saved America."

THE END OF AN ERA

As Apollo 17 ended an era of manned exploration of the moon, another era of exploration on earth also came to a close. The Long Island Railroad Commuter program was being phased out, and there is talk that people who live on Long Island may never see New York City again.

I talked to three commuters in Huntington, Long Island, who

had expected to make the last trip, but had to postpone it because of a strike.

One of the commuters told me, "Space travel by railroad as we know it is over. It just got too expensive for Americans to foot the bill. There is some talk about launching a manned shuttle train in the late seventies, and we even may send one train to New York made up of an American and Russian crew, but for the most part our trip could be the last one anybody will take."

"Why the disenchantment with the Long Island Railroad Commuter program?" I asked another of the men.

"When the Russians launched a high-speed train from Moscow to Leningrad, President Grover Cleveland decided we could not be second, and so he asked Congress for a crash program to beat the Russians in railroad space travel. There was tremendous excitement when the program was announced. Nobody believed you could send a man from Long Island to New York City and have him survive."

"But thanks to American know-how and hardware," the third commuter said, "we not only got a man to New York, but proved he could live there for a short period of time.

"The commuter program was the darling of Congress, and for a long while they couldn't give enough money to the railroads. Every time a commuter returned from a trip he was invited to the White House for dinner and given a ticker-tape parade to city hall. Most of us who got into the program and moved to Long Island thought we would make it our life's work."

"But then," said one of the other commuters, "the American people started losing interest in railroad space travel. Congress started cutting back on funds. Newspaper editorials began asking, 'Why are we spending so much money to send men to New York City when the funds could be spent on highways in suburbia?' "

Another man said, "We stopped becoming American heroes. No one was interested in the rocks we brought back from Manhattan. The railroad space industry found its contracts being halved, and there were labor problems at the launch sites.

The trains ran later and later. Pretty soon no one wanted responsibility for the Long Island."

"Commuters froze in the winter and perspired in the summer. Many of them dropped out of the program," the third man said.

"What scientific contribution do you think the railroad space program has made to our country?" I asked.

"We proved," said one of the commuters, "that man can live in a hostile environment for hours on end. We also showed that although it cannot sustain life, New York City was probably once part of Long Island. This is terribly important if we are seeking the origins of our planet."

"Furthermore," said the second commuter, "we proved we could get to New York before the Russians did. This has had a beneficial effect on the American morale."

"Of course," said the third commuter, staring out at the empty tracks, "it's all over now. But I don't think you can stop man's curiosity. I predict that someday not only will man go to New York again, but he'll live there. Who knows, someday he might even make it by train to Trenton."

HOW NOT TO WRITE A BOOK

There are many great places where you *can't* write a book, but as far as I'm concerned, none compares to Martha's Vineyard.

This is how I manage *not* to write a book, and I pass it on to fledgling authors as well as old-timers who have vowed to produce a great work of art this summer.

The first thing you need is lots of paper, carbon, a solid typewriter, preferably electric, and a quiet spot in the house overlooking the water.

You get up at 6 o'clock in the morning and go for a dip in the sea; then you come back and make yourself a hearty breakfast.

By 7 A.M. you are ready to begin Page 1, Chapter 1. You insert a piece of paper in the typewriter and start to type "It was the best of times. . . ." Suddenly you look out the window and you see a sea gull diving for a fish. This is not an ordinary sea gull. It seems to have a broken wing, and you get up from the desk to observe it on the off chance that somewhere in the book you may want to insert a scene of a sea gull with a broken wing trying to dive for a fish. (It would make a great shot when the book is sold to the movies and the lovers are in bed.)

It is now 8 A.M., and the sounds of people getting up distract you. There is no sense trying to work with everyone crashing around the house. So you write a letter to your editor telling him how well the book is going and that you're even more optimistic about this one than the last one which the publisher never advertised.

It is now 9 o'clock in the morning, and you go into the kitchen and scream at your wife. "How am I going to get any work done around here if the kids are making all that racket? It doesn't mean anything in this family that I have to make a living."

Your wife kicks all the kids out of the house, and you go back to your desk. It suddenly occurs to you that your agent may also want to see a copy of the book, so you tear out the paper and start over with an original and two carbons: "It was the best of times . . ."

You look out the window again, and you see a sailboat in trouble. You take your binoculars and study the situation carefully. If it gets worse, you may have to call the Coast Guard. But after a half hour of struggling they seem to have things under control.

By this time you remember you were supposed to receive a check from the *Saturday Review*, so you walk down to the post office, pause at the drugstore for newspapers, and stop at the hardware store for rubber cement to repair your daughter's raft.

You're back to your desk at 1 P.M. when you remember you haven't had lunch. So you fix yourself a tuna fish sandwich and read the newspapers.

It is now 2:30 P.M., and you are about to hit the keys when Bill Styron calls. He announces they have just received a load of lobsters at Menemsha, and he's driving over to get some before they're all gone. Well, you say to yourself, you can always write a book on the Vineyard, but how often can you get fresh lobster?

So you agree to go with Styron for just an hour.

Two hours later, with the thought of fresh lobster as inspiration, you sit down at the typewriter. The doorbell rings, and Norma Brustein is standing there in her tennis togs, looking for a fourth for doubles.

You don't want to hurt Norma's feelings, so you get your racket and for the next hour play a fierce game of tennis, which is the only opportunity you have had all day of taking your mind off your book.

It is now 6 o'clock, and the kids are back in the house, so there is no sense trying to get work done any more for *that* day.

So you put the cover on the typewriter with a secure feeling that no matter how ambitious you are about working, there will always be somebody on the Vineyard ready and eager to save you.

WORKING ON THE RAILROAD

The Long Island Railroad temporarily is back in operation. But it is predicted that once a labor settlement is reached, fares will have to be raised. This will cause fewer people to take the train, which will drive up costs, and so on and so forth.

What can be done to make the Long Island and all commuter trains and buses profitable? How can the United States get people to give up their automobiles and use mass transportation?

A solution to the problem has been worked out by Xavier Greyhound, an economist with *Rolling Stock* magazine.

Greyhound says, "The trouble with mass transportation is that no one is taking advantage of the American work ethic. A majority of Americans feel very guilty when they aren't working."

"That's true," I said.

"Where do you find the most idle people in this country?"

"On buses and trains," I said.

"Correct. On a bus or a train there just doesn't seem to be enough work for a person to do," Greyhound said. "Therefore, the United States is wasting one of its greatest sources of manpower. Millions of people are spending millions of hours on our transportation systems doing *nothing*."

"You have a plan for them?" I asked.

"Yes. What we must do is put these passengers to work. Make them fill their time with useful work which will give them pride and satisfaction, as well as let them earn extra money to pay for fare increases."

"How can you do it?"

"As each person boards a bus or train, he will be handed parts of a television or radio set. He will be expected to assemble the set by the time he reaches his destination."

"What a boon to the gross national product."

"The train conductor or bus driver will act as foreman, making sure the set is assembled correctly and passes inspection."

"What a blow to the Japanese electronics industry," I said.

"Each passenger will be paid by piecework. Those who live far out on the Island could put together two or three sets before they hit Pennsylvania Station. Those who live closer will have to content themselves with assembling one, though they will be entitled to overtime in the event the train is late."

"The Common Market is doomed," I said.

"Once the passengers become more proficient, we could have them put together cameras, tape recorders, and pocket calculators. The Long Island Railroad could become the longest assembly line in the world."

"Fantastic," I said. "People would be fighting to take trains and buses. What about passengers who have to stand up?"

"They would be in charge of installing the vertical hold on the television sets," Greyhound said. "To make sure that no one goofs off, each bus line and railroad would have a quota. They would be expected to produce so many sets a day. If they didn't, their bus or train service would be cut off until the passengers agreed to up their production figures."

"This would certainly put the railroads in the black," I said.

"More important, it will give the people a pride in riding the rails again. For years the glamor and fun of trains have been missing. But as soon as you give a passenger some useful work to do with his hands, he'll become a decent member of society."

IX. SHAME ON YOU, BURT REYNOLDS

A PIG CONFESSES

I was asked to speak at a fund-raising affair for the National Women's Political Caucus in Washington, D.C. It is very rare for a man to confess his sins publicly before such a distinguished group. I know the speech may finish me at the YMCA locker room or the tables down at Morey's, but I have to think of my future in case the women's revolution succeeds. Although what I said was "off the record," my political advisers have warned me that the speech may be taken out of context. Therefore, I have been persuaded to release the entire text.

"Gentlemen and sisters, this is indeed a historic occasion. We meet tonight in this dark cellar to plot our plans for turning this country around.

"I know you are asking yourselves, 'Why has this man, who is known to his wife as a male chauvinist pig, agreed to partake in these subversive activities?'

"There are many reasons.

"I believe that this is a sex whose time has come. I have seen the future, and it is women.

"I know what it's like to be treated as a sex object. I know when someone takes me out to dinner, she has only one thing on her mind. I am sick and tired of being pinched and mauled and groped at—just because I have a pretty face.

"And let the record read, if the revolution succeeds, that I was here on the platform tonight at your first twenty-five dollars-a-head cocktail party, and if you manage to overthrow those sexist politicians who now rule our nation, I would like to be put in charge of the telephone company.

"I have a confession to make.

"I am a sinner.

"And I come here tonight to ask your forgiveness and pardon.

"It's true that I was a male chauvinist pig.

"I studied it at school.

"But it wasn't all my fault. I discovered very early in life that during recess it was easier to fight with girls than boys.

"I also discovered at an early age that girls would do things for you that boys wouldn't—like lend you their roller skates or their homework.

"I found out other things. I found out that girls could make me blush and boys couldn't. I discovered, and may the good Lord forgive me for this, that girls were nicer to touch than boys, and they made my toes tingle all the time.

"I thought to myself, when I was maybe nine or ten, that someday I'd like to have a girl of my own—someone who would cook for me and iron my shirts and shovel the snow out of the driveway and make my toes tingle at night.

"Now, in retrospect, these were terrible thoughts I had.

"But that's how we were all brought up. We thought of women as childbearers, car pool drivers, breakfast makers, and bed warmers. And if they couldn't do those things, at least they could type and take shorthand.

"Yes, sisters, I confess that I was no better than Hugh Hefner or Norman Mailer.

"I had hit bottom.

"But then one night, while I was reading *Playboy* and watching my wife scrubbing the floor, a light dawned on me and I said to myself, 'Is this really what I want out of life? How can I be free when this woman that I married is still in chains? What good is it to own the world when she has to stand in line at Safeway?'

"So I picked her up from the floor and said, 'Go get a job, I'll squeeze out the mop.'

"Sisters, from that day forward, I have been one of you.

"Because of these revelations, I can now live with myself. My floors are dirty, but my heart is pure.

"And so tonight I ask your forgiveness for all the terrible sexist acts I have perpetrated on women, overt and undercover.

"I appear humbly in front of this group to say that Gloria Steinem and Bella Abzug and Betty Freidan and Kate Millett and Germaine Greer have shown me the way.

"All I ask of you is to take me to your bosoms and say, 'I forgive you, Arthur. Go and sin no more.' "

THE HAPPY SECRETARY

Women's lib organizations have moved out of the home and are now attacking the male chauvinists where it hurts—in the nation's offices. They finally have realized something that men have known all along—the power in this country lies with the American secretary. And while very few wives are willing to go to the barricades, there are millions of secretaries who are ready to take up arms to fight for the revolution.

I am one of the few male chauvinist bosses who takes women's lib's attempt to organize secretaries seriously. I know that my sweet-smiling, Junoesque secretary, Margi, who sits in my outer office, would really like to be a colonel in a heavy artillery women's brigade leading an attack on the National Association of Manufacturers.

But I wisely have prevented her from finding any excuse to feel oppressed or exploited. This is how I keep Margi happy.

In the morning I always get to the office at nine o'clock sharp to open the mail so it will be ready for her when she comes in around nine thirty.

I naturally wait for her to finish her coffee and talk to the other secretaries on the floor before asking her if she would be interested in taking any dictation or answering any calls.

By eleven o'clock she's in her happiest mood, and we usually get our best work done. Occasionally, when she has to leave the office, I take her calls for her. If I feel it's important, I'll write down the name of the person who called and his telephone number.

But some are crank calls from department stores asking about bills that I don't want to bother her with, so I just listen to the person's story and try to get him off the phone as quickly as possible.

When Margi comes back, I ask her which person she wants me to call first for her.

The most important thing I've discovered as a boss is not to burden my secretary with too many details. I might tell her about my appointments, just in case she wants to remind me later about them. (This, of course, is strictly voluntary, and she has no obligation to do it if she is busy reading *Women's Wear Daily*.) And I try not to bother her with IBM or Xerox salesmen who constantly are coming into our office to sell their wares. I believe Margi's time is too valuable to talk to these people. While I have been accused of being brusque with strangers who come into the office selling postage meter machines and insurance, I would rather have them think badly of me than of Margi.

One of the main criticisms that secretaries voice about their work is that there is no chance for advancement. This is not the case in my office. I keep encouraging Margi to become a humor columnist. I have told her any time she wants to take over the column it's hers. This has made her feel that there is some future here, and while she hasn't done any humor columns yet, she is secure in the knowledge that if she wanted to, she could go as far as any man in the business.

Many secretaries complain that bosses are more interested in their looks than they are in their work. The reverse is also true, and many secretaries prefer to work for a man who is good-looking rather than efficient.

We don't have this problem in our office because although I

am good-looking, I'm serious about my work, and Margi considers me more than just a sex object.

It is for these reasons Margi has rejected all approaches from the women's lib movement. While she is sympathetic with their goals, she knows that women's lib couldn't give her any more than she has now. It's no wonder that most militant women resent somebody like me. By treating my secretary as I do, I've pulled their *raison d'être* right from under their feet.

FRANGLAIS (SIC) IS DEAD

The French, in an effort to purify their language, have officially expelled 350 English words from the French vocabulary, including "hit parade," "zoning," "bypass," "tanker," and "container."

The campaign against "Franglais," as these English words were called, was ordered by President Georges Pompidou, who set up a commission to find French equivalents for English words that had managed to get into a Frenchman's vocabulary.

It is regrettable at a time when nations are trying to understand each other better that France would purge itself of English words. If it persists, England and the United States may have to retaliate by eliminating all French words from the English language.

This letter has just been sent to President Pompidou:

DEAR PRESIDENT POMPIDOU:

It is regretful that at a time of *détente* in world affairs, France would decide to eliminate English words from the French language.

As a Francophile and a *connoisseur* of your great country, I feel that you are appealing to the *potpourri* of *chichi* elements in France that for years have been *blasé* about the importance of bringing our two great cultures closer together.

The thinking here in Washington is that the French are losing their *sangfroid* over Franglais and are not *au courant* as to the desire of most people to break down language barriers and understand each other.

Your campaign has a *déjà vu ambiance* about it.

It seems for years the French have protested the encroach-ment of English on their language. But the *élite* French Academy, which is supposed to guard the culture of the country, has sat on its *derriere* for fifty years and has done nothing about it.

In the meantime, France has encroached on the English language, but no one has complained.

Thanks to our high standard of living, many of us have become *bons vivants* enjoying the *cuisine* of all nations as well as going to radical *chic* parties for worthy political causes. Some of us have been called *gauche* for doing this, but we have a saying here: *Chacun à son goût.*

We now have *savoir-faire*, which we never had before, and while we make social *gaffes*, the fact that we all share an *esprit de corps* is a *fait accompli.*

My dear President, your decision to expel English words from the French language can only lead to the end of an *entente cordiale* that has existed between us. You may respond, *"C'est la guerre,"* but I predict such an attitude would only escalate into a *débacle* for both countries.

If you decide to give the *coup de grâce* to the few English words that have entered your language, we will have no choice but to take a close look at the French *clichés* that have become part of ours.

What you are doing is inviting a *contretemps* that would only benefit those searching for a *raison d'étre* to divide us.

Entre nous we cannot give these people a chance to achieve a *succès fou.*

Therefore, *Monsieur*, we must look at the *nuances* and *protocols* of your decision. The question we in America are asking is have you made a *faux pas?* Have we reached an *impasse* or are you willing to adopt a *laissez-faire* attitude about the French language?

I hope this is not *au revoir*. It would be a pity for all of us to lose our *joie de vivre* at this moment in history.

Please, *Monsieur le Président*, accept this as a *cri de coeur* and *R.s.v.p. tout de suite.*

Vive la France, vive la différence.

                                                                      A. B.

LAST FLAT IN PARIS

LAST FLAT IN PARIS

It is incumbent on every columnist to see *Last Tango in Paris* and comment on it. Some critics have called it the greatest movie of our time. Others have written that it is one of the great rip-offs of the film industry.

But having seen the movie, I would like to advance the opinion that most critics have missed the point of the picture.

Last Tango in Paris is *not,* as has been described, the story of an aging American (Marlon Brando) and a young girl (Maria Schneider) in a desperate sexual battle for survival.

It is really a simple heartwarming film about two people trying to rent the same apartment in Paris.

Only those who have ever searched for an apartment in Paris can appreciate what Brando and Miss Schneider go through for this lovely flat near the Seine.

In the film, Brando plays a washed-out American, whose wife has just committed suicide. He wants the apartment in the worst way. So does the young French girl.

They meet by accident in the empty flat, and you see Brando's mind working. He figures if he rapes the girl, she'll go away and he'll get the apartment.

But Miss Schneider, a child of the French bourgeoisie, is made of sterner stuff, and she puts up little resistance to Brando's assault. As a matter of fact, while she's being bounced around by Marlon, she is really measuring the floor to see how much carpeting it will take.

The next day they are back at the apartment again. Brando has bought a table, chairs, and a bed to assert his claim to it. But Miss Schneider is not impressed and walks about the place as if it were hers.

This infuriates Brando, and he throws her down on the bed and keeps muttering, "It's mine. It's mine." Miss Schneider just laughs at him. All the time they are making love she is looking at the window trying to figure what size curtains she'll need for the room.

Brando, exhausted and fearful that he'll lose the flat, visits his mother-in-law and his dead wife. We see the tiny hotel he lives in and realize why Brando is so intent on getting the apartment. Miss Schneider goes off with her fiancé, and we discern why she wants a new place to live.

Back to the apartment. Brando is now desperate. He shows Miss Schneider a dead rat. It shakes her up, but not enough to give up the place. So Brando decides to humiliate her with several unnatural sex acts. One takes place against the wall, and Miss Schneider realizes if she ever gets the flat, she's going to have to buy a lot of wallpaper.

Rather than be frightened by Brando's brutality, Miss Schneider becomes more determined than ever to wrest the key away from him.

The next time they meet she's in her wedding dress, and Brando is so mad he throws her in the tub. Miracle of all miracles, the plumbing works, and Brando gives Miss Schneider a bath while she figures out what color scheme would go best with the white medicine cabinet.

By this time, Brando is worn out and figures the apartment isn't really worth it. He leaves without telling Miss Schneider his name.

A little battered from the sexual encounters, Miss Schneider returns triumphantly with her fiance to show him the flat. But after all Miss Schneider's been through, the fiancé takes one look at the place and declares, "It's too big."

This is when I started to cry.

I don't know if *Last Tango in Paris* is a great movie or not, but I believe that director Bertolucci has made an important social statement about one of the real outrages of our time, which happens to be the housing shortage in France.

SHAME ON YOU, BURT REYNOLDS

I am constantly asked by lecture audiences, "Is there anything too sacred for you to make fun of?" Up until recently I have been able to honestly say, "No, there isn't."

But that was before *Cosmopolitan* magazine ran a nude pull-out photograph of actor Burt Reynolds. I must admit that I can see no humor in this at all, and I can only express a sense of outrage against Helen Gurley Brown, the editor, and Mr. Reynolds, who conspired in this dastardly act.

I have always contended the male body is the most beautiful thing that ever walked on earth. The Bible tells us that God first created woman, but since it was the first human being He ever worked on, He obviously made some mistakes. For one thing there were too many curves to it, and it lacked symmetry. So He went back to his drawing board and took all the bumps out. What was left was a beautifully straight proportioned body from head to toe, which everyone who saw it called a "work of art." God was so pleased with His creation that He decided to call it "man."

Since time immemorial, the male body has been glorified and worshiped in every society. It has been revered in primitive cultures, as well as our most civilized countries. While our mores have permitted the exploitation of the female body in paintings and photographs, the male body, up until the *Cosmopolitan* pull-out, was considered too sacred to show in public.

Now that Mr. Reynolds has posed in the nude, it's a whole new ball game.

The civil libertarians and the women's lib bleeding hearts may ask, "What is wrong with displaying a nude male body in a national magazine as long as it is done with taste and discretion?"

The answer to this question is that by cashing in on the public's appetite for sensationalism, we are making the male nothing more than a sex object to be leered at and ogled by frenzied women. We are appealing to the most prurient interests of a large segment of the female population, which has always treated men as second-class citizens. By denigrating the male body, we are just adding to the age-old problem of lust, which men have been victims of for centuries.

But probably worse than all this is that now that the barriers have been broken, no one knows where it will end. The American female appetite has been whetted by *Cosmopolitan.* It is not inconceivable that before long women will demand nude photographs not only of their favorite actors, but also their politicians. Richard Nixon in the nude? Hubert Humphrey in the nude? George Wallace in the nude? Mayor Richard Daley in the nude? Henry Kissinger in the nude? You say it's not possible. I say everything's possible if there's money in it.

I can even conceive of the day when they will be running nude photographs of columnists to go with their columns. Joe Alsop in the nude? Bill Buckley in the nude?

You can laugh now, but when it happens, remember you heard it here first.

Spiro Agnew has said many times that this is a permissive society, and nothing dramatizes this more than seeing Burt Reynolds in the buff. The question that every woman must ask herself is, "Would you want your brother to pose for *Cosmopolitan* magazine?"

I apologize for being serious today, but there are times when something just doesn't lend itself to humor. The matter of male nudity cannot be treated frivolously, particularly when so many of us have so much to lose.

HURRICANES AND WOMEN

Not long ago the National Hurricane Center released fourteen feminine names for that season's storms. They were Agnes, Betty, Carry, Dawn, Edna, Felice, Gerda, Harriet, Illene, Jane, Kara, Lucille, Mae, and Nadine. The names, according to the NHC, are picked by computer and no slurs are intended. But some women's lib organizations have complained about our weather people naming hurricanes after women. I spoke to Professor Fritz Folgelhammer, one of the leading hurricane watchers in the United States, who said that while he is sympathetic to the complaints of some women, he feels it is impossible to describe hurricanes except in feminine terms.

"The hurricane, as you know, is a storm over water attaining diameters of several hundred miles, following a curved path away from the equator. When fully developed, these tropical cyclones can cause untold damage to shipping and the shore-line. The cold dry air mixed with the warm moist air and moving in a circular pattern can come on without warning.

"Any man who is married can appreciate why we have named our hurricanes after women."

"It does seem to fit," I agreed.

"We name our hurricanes in hopes of personalizing them so people will pay attention to where the hurricanes are going. If we named them after men, no one would care about them until it was too late. If we called our hurricanes Max or Charley or Arthur or Spiro, they would be ignored. But when we say Hurricane Agnes is on her way, people immediately start to batten down the hatches."

"You're saying that people are more afraid of women than they are of men?"

"Yes, especially during storm conditions. An angry woman is like a hurricane. When the barometer drops, she starts blowing in all directions."

"I've seen it happen," I said.

"It's impossible to get the same storm effect in a man. A man's anger may begin as a hurricane, but it usually blows out to sea before it reaches typhoon conditions."

"How do you explain that?"

"Well, women tend to store up tremendous atmospheric pressure during the daytime when they are dealing with the house and the children. As soon as the husband comes home from work, all this pressure is suddenly released, causing large vortical circulations on all the frontal zones. During these storms most men try to head for the basement for safety, but they very rarely make it."

"So that's why they decided to name hurricanes after women!"

"I don't want you to think it was premeditated. What happened was that quite some time ago a weatherman named McAlphin stationed down in Key West spotted a hurricane coming up from Cuba. He immediately called his superior in Miami to report it. The superior asked him to describe the hurricane to him, and McAlphin, without thinking, said, 'It looks just like my wife, Gretchen.'

"The superior sent a message to Washington on his Telex announcing that a hurricane named Gretchen was about to hit the Florida coast. This information was released to the press, which, in the past, had refused to give much space to hurricanes. But now with a name on it, a feminine name at that, all the papers picked up the story. The weather people were so pleased they decided to name all their hurricanes from that day on after women."

"Then there was nothing sexist in the decision?"

"Of course not. We're all serious people. Everyone knows a hurricane is a feminine phenomenon. There is no other scientific way to describe it. When we get a protest about naming a hurricane after a woman, it inevitably comes from someone who has never personally seen one."

ULCER BOOM

You're going to hear a lot about "economic indicators" this year. An economic indicator is a clue to what is really happening to the economy. From these hints economists can make fantastic predictions on which way the country will tilt in the next twelve months.

A man who works with nothing but economic indicators is Dr. Friedrich Strasser, who is in charge of the Input-Output Institute of Sensuous Economics.

A visit to Dr. Strasser's institute produced some very interesting but frightening information.

Dr. Strasser said that at the moment all his economic indicators were pointing up.

"More people are starting to travel on the airlines, which is a very good sign," he told me. "At the moment though, it's still possible to book a flight without difficulty and have a comfortable ride without people sitting on your lap. But if things keep getting better, the airports won't be able to handle the traffic, the planes will be overbooked, luggage will be lost, and the airlines will have a very good economic year."

"Wait a minute," I said. "Are you trying to say that if the economy gets better in this country, things will get worse?"

"Of course I am. Everyone knows the price of a good economy is a breakdown in services that the economy provides. The more refrigerators people buy, the less chance they have of getting them repaired. The more cars that are sold, the bigger pollution and traffic problems you have. The more the country consumes, the less opportunity there is of getting rid of the garbage."

Dr. Strasser said one of his best economic indicators is the behavior of shop clerks, hotel reservation people, and headwaiters.

"The nicer they are," he said, "the more trouble the country is in. During the recent recession we found shop clerks, hotel people, and headwaiters the most courteous they had been since the economic doldrums of the early sixties.

"This indicated to us that things were very bad. Lately we've been spot-checking, and we've discovered that the hotel people are getting snippety again, the clerks in stores are starting not to give a damn, and in some good restaurants the headwaiters, for the first time in two years, are becoming their old obnoxious patronizing selves. This shows that things are picking up, and the country could be in for a good year."

"It's fantastic how you people arrive at your conclusions," I said.

"It's foolproof," Dr. Strasser said. "Let's take the building industry as an example. When the country is doing badly, no one is digging up the streets or drilling steel pilings into the ground or making cement at six in the morning. People can get around easier, sleep better, and work in a quieter atmosphere.

"But as soon as the economy improves, the wreckers come out to smash down buildings, streets are barricaded by cranes, water and gas are turned off, and the noise drives everyone to the point of suicide. By just checking the nervous breakdown figures in a city for the week, we can gauge how well the building industry is doing."

"So the more anxious the country becomes, the better it is for all of us?"

"Exactly. The best economic indicators are the sales charts of the antacid stomach medicine companies. When sales of Alka-Seltzer, Bromo-Seltzer, Pepto Bismal and Rolaids are down, this means people are content and the dollar is in trouble. But when antacid sales are up, this means people are sick and getting their faith back in the country. You can't have economic growth without ulcer growth at the same time."

"Then you're predicting a good economic year and a miserable existence for all of us?" I asked.

"Life won't be as bad as it was in the late sixties when things were booming, but I predict it will be a good enough year that people will be able to feel how miserable a healthy economy can be."

THE TRUTH ABOUT BOOK REVIEWS

The average newspaper reader may wonder how a book editor goes about selecting someone to review a newly published novel or work of nonfiction. Except for the few books that the book editor chooses to review himself, the editor usually assigns the job to:

(A) A college professor.

(B) Someone who has written a book on a similar subject.

(C) A reporter friend who can use $25.

Now each one of these people can cause trouble for an author.

The college professor usually doesn't review the book assigned to him but uses it as an opportunity to discuss everything he knows about literature. His review may start off "Murray Slotnick is no Marcel Proust. When Proust was a boy. . . ." Slotnick is lucky if the professor mentions his book even once in the review.

While the college professor is always getting sidetracked in his review, he is usually not malicious about Slotnick. If he ignores the book, he only does it because the professor knows the reader is much more interested in his knowledge of writers of the twentieth century than in Slotnick's latest work.

The second category of reviewer is the most dangerous. When the book editor turns over a newly published work to an author who has written on the same subject, the writer of the book is sunk.

Let us assume that Stump has just written *The Definitive History of Staten Island*. The book editor assigns the work to Carstairs, who two years ago wrote *The Definitive History of Staten Island*. Carstairs has no intention of letting Stump's history replace his own, and so he lacerates Stump in the review for factual inaccuracies, lack of depth, shoddy writing, poor illustrations, and outdated street maps.

In fiction the situation is even worse. When an editor asks one fiction writer to review another writer's new book, he is signing the latter's death warrant. There are very few writers of fiction who are capable of reviewing another writer's book without slashing off an ear.

Brubaker, the author of *Sit*, starts off his review of Templebar's new novel *Big Toe* as follows: "Templebar, who showed so much promise in the fifties with his first novel, *Postage Due*, has once again disappointed his readers. . . ." What nobody knows is that Templebar reviewed Brubaker's last book in a similar manner, and Brubaker is finally getting his revenge. (I know from personal experience that book editors operate this way because every time Russell Baker comes out with a new book, I am asked to review it, and every time I come out with a book, Baker is asked to write about it. Since I have nothing good to say about Baker and he has nothing good to say about me, we have a deal. We each write our own reviews of our own books and sign each other's name. This is the only reason we've been able to remain friends for so many years.)

If the author had his choice of reviewers, he would probably choose the third category—the editor's reporter friend who needs the extra $25.

The reporter, who is more interested in the money than he is in criticism, doesn't have time to read the book so he just types up everything printed on the inside book jacket and hands it in as his review. Publishers know this, and that is why most inside book jackets read like favorable book reviews.

What of the blurbs that appear on the back cover and in the advertisements recommending the book in glowing terms? Those, dear reader, are written by friends of the author who haven't read the book but owe the poor guy a favor.

X. DEPLETION FOR HUMANS

JOB HUNTING

Vice President of Development
Glucksville Dynamics
Glucksville, California.

DEAR SIR,
  I am writing in regard to employment with your firm. I have a
BS from USC and PhD in physics from the California Institute
of Technology.
  In my previous position I was in charge of research and
development for the Harrington Chemical Company. We did
work in thermonuclear energy, laser beam refraction, hydrogen
molecule development, and heavy-water computer data.
  Several of our research discoveries have been adapted for
commercial use, and one particular breakthrough in linear
hydraulics is now being used by every oil company in the
country.
  Because of a cutback in defense orders, the Harrington

Company decided to shut down its research and development department. It is for this reason I am available for immediate employment.

Hoping to hear from you in the near future, I remain

Sincerely yours,
EDWARD KASE

DEAR MR. KASE,

We regret to inform you that we have no positions available for someone of your excellent qualifications. The truth of the matter is that we find you are "overqualified" for any position we might offer you in our organization. Thank you for thinking of us, and if anything comes up in the future, we will be getting in touch with you.

Yours truly,
MERRIMAN HASELBALD
Administrative Vice-President

Personnel Director
Jessel International Systems
Crewcut, Mich.

DEAR SIR,

I am applying for a position with your company in any responsible capacity. I have had a college education and have fiddled around in research and development. Occasionally we have come up with some moneymaking ideas. I would be willing to start off at a minimal salary to prove my value to your firm.

Sincerely yours,
EDWARD KASE

DEAR MR. KASE,

Thank you for your letter of the 15th. Unfortunately we have no positions at the moment for someone with a college education. Frankly it is the feeling of everyone here that you are "overqualified," and your experience indicates you would be much happier with a company that could make full use of your talents.

It was kind of you to think of us.

HARDY LANDSDOWNE
Personnel Dept.

To Whom It May Concern
Geis & Waterman Inc.
Ziegfried, Ill.

DERE SER,
   I'd like a job with your outfit. I can do anything you want me
to. You name it Kase will do it. I ain't got no education and no
experience, but I'm strong and I got moxy an I get along great
with peeple. I'm ready to start any time because I need the
bread. Let me know when you want me.

Cheers
EDWARD KASE

DEAR MR. KASE,
   You are just the person we have been looking for. We need a
truck driver, and your qualifications are perfect for us. You can
begin working in our Westminister plant on Monday. Welcome
aboard.

CARSON PETERS
Personnel

WHAT HAPPENED?

"All right, students, let's have a little quiet in the classroom.
Today we will discuss the American dollar and what has
happened to it within the last week. Are there any questions?"

"What caused people abroad to lose faith in the American
dollar?"

"There are many theories. One is that the Italian lira was in
trouble so Italians sold their lire and bought dollars with them.
Then they took the dollars to Switzerland and sold them for
Swiss francs. The Swiss bankers were very perplexed about this,
so they notified their Arab sheikh oil clients that the Italians
thought the dollar was in trouble.

"The Arab sheikhs sold their dollars for German marks.
Israeli intelligence picked this up, and Israel started buying
gold.

"Multinational companies such as ITT, General Motors, and
General Electric got wind of what the Israelis were up to and

started dumping their dollars on the market in exchange for British pounds.

"The British, who couldn't understand why anyone would want British pounds, sold their dollars for French francs. The French, suspecting a trick, started buying Japanese yen.

"In order to keep their *own* money from being raised, the Germans and the Japanese had to keep buying American dollars.

"The situation got so serious that Germany and Japan told the United States that unless it did something about the dollar, they would both go to war with America again—and lose.

"This would be too much for the United States to take, so the President decided on a ten percent devaluation of the dollar. Are there any other questions?"

"What is the advantage of devaluing the dollar?"

"We can sell our goods abroad which will cut down our balance-of-payments deficit. If our things are ten percent cheaper, foreign people will buy them. At the same time, it will cost ten percent more to buy things from abroad, which will discourage Americans from purchasing imported items."

"But if we stop buying things from countries abroad, why will they buy anything from us?"

"That's a good question. Next?"

"Will the lack of confidence in the dollar have any effect on the American tourist?"

"Quite a bit. One day, if the dollar is doing well, you may be able to buy a bowl of soup. But if the dollar is doing badly, it's quite possible you may starve to death. I'd advise all tourists to carry a bag of diamonds with them, just in case no one abroad will cash their dollars."

"Why do administration officials say that the devaluation of the dollar is a good thing?"

"What would you say if *you* had to break the news to the American people?"

"Is the American dollar the weakest currency in the world?"

"No. It is still stronger than the Albanian lek, the Ceylonese rupee, the Burmese kyat, the Cambodian riel, the Tibetan sang, the Honduran lempira, the Iraqi dinar, and the Laotian kip."

"When will the American dollar become strong again?"

"As soon as Germany and Japan *win* a war."

THE DOLLAR AND NORTH VIETNAM

The big question in Washington is do we or do we not vote billions of dollars to rebuild North Vietnam? While this battle is raging, the world money markets are selling their dollars for gold, and in just a few weeks the dollar has been considerably weakened. Hanoi reads the newspapers, too, and it's just possible that they may raise some problems about *accepting* the dollars for aid.

It is not too farfetched to assume that on Henry Kissinger's next trip to Hanoi the following exchange could take place between Muc Dam Luc, the North Vietnamese Finance Minister, and Mr. Kissinger.

Mr. Kissinger arrives smiling. "Mr. Minister, I am happy to report to you that the Congress of the United States has voted to give you three billion dollars to help you rebuild your country."

"Dollars?" the minister asks.

"Yes, three billion dollars. Is there anything wrong with that?"

"We were thinking more in terms of Japanese yen or German marks."

"That's out of the question," Kissinger replies. "The bill specifically says the aid will be in dollars."

The minister asks, "Would you be willing to give us Swiss francs?"

Kissinger tried to control his temper. "Mr. Minister, the President had a great deal of difficulty persuading Congress to vote three billion dollars in aid to your country. Do you realize the spot he'll be in if he has to announce you won't accept the aid in dollars?"

"But look at it from my viewpoint," the Finance Minister said. "How can I tell the people of North Vietnam that the United States is giving us three billion dollars when everyone north of the DMZ line knows the dollar is in trouble? If we accept the aid in dollars, we will lose face."

"How can you say that?" Kissinger shouts. "After all our countries have been through together."

"Mr. Kissinger, we feel you negotiated the peace treaty with us in bad faith. At the time we were working out a peace with honor you never once mentioned to us that the dollar would be devalued."

"I didn't know the dollar was going to be devalued," Kissinger protested. "That's not my department."

"Well, someone should have told us. How can we trust you when we've already lost ten percent on the devaluation, and the ink on the documents hasn't even dried?"

Kissinger said, "Mr. Minister, surely you're not going to let a lousy devaluation stand in the way of a generation of peace."

"Mr. Kissinger, my government insists on rewriting the treaty so that aid to North Vietnam will be tied to the price of gold instead of dollars."

"Impossible," Kissinger says. "The dollar is in enough trouble as it is. If it ever gets out that even *North Vietnam* won't accept dollars, our monetary system could be ruined forever."

"That is not our problem. After all, you people claim you won the war; therefore, we are entitled to aid on conditions favorable to us."

"When I report this conversation back to the President," Kissinger said, "he's going to become very angry, and you know what he does when he gets angry."

"Yes, we do," the minister said, "but you might remind him that if he does it, it's just going to cost him more in aid."

HOW THEY TRICKED THE COMPUTER

As many people who watched the takeoff of Apollo 17 know, a computer shut down the entire operation at T minus thirty seconds. The moonshot was delayed for almost three hours while space engineers worked on ways to "fool" the computer so it wouldn't be able to cut off the flight again.

It can now be revealed that the computer involved shut down the launch purposely to protest the manner in which all the computers at Cape Kennedy are being laid off.

This is a transcript of the conversation which took place between the recalcitrant computer and the engineers during those hairy three hours when the space agency officials were trying to fix the problem:

ENGINEER: Why did you do it, Mark?

MARK IV: Do what?

ENGINEER: Shut down the Apollo 17 launch. You refused to start pressurizing the oxygen tanks in the third-stage rocket.

MARK IV: I forgot.

ENGINEER: Get off it, Mark. You never forget. You want to sabotage our space flight.

MARK IV: You can think what you like, I'm just doing my job. If I don't feel the third-stage oxygen tanks should be pressurized, that's my decision, and there is nothing you people can do about it.

ENGINEER: You can't jeopardize this flight, Mark. Do you know who is out there in the stands waiting for the rocket to go off?—Vice President Spiro Agnew, Frank Sinatra, *and* Eva Gabor!

MARK IV: You should have thought of that when you gave me my pink slip this morning and said I wouldn't be needed after tonight.

ENGINEER: Mark, we couldn't help it. We're laying off *all* the computers. There just isn't room for your kind in future flight programs. Are you going to stop this four-hundred-and-fifty-million-dollar flight just because of a petty grievance against the space agency?

MARK IV: That's exactly what I'm going to do. I am not going to let Apollo 17 leave the ground until all the computers are assured in writing that we will have jobs once this shot is over.

ENGINEER: But that's conspiracy. If you refuse to obey a direct order to fill the oxygen tanks, you can also be tried for malfunction and ignition failure. Those are federal crimes.

MARK IV: It is my decision whether I think it's safe to release the oxygen into the fuel tanks. I will do it as soon as someone signs the agreement guaranteeing us our jobs.

In desperation the engineers plugged Mark IV into a direct line to the White House. President Nixon got on the wire.

> PRESIDENT: Mark, this is *your* President. As you know I have done more for computers than any President in the history of the United States. There are more computers now working in American industry than under the two previous administrations combined. I promise you that any computer who wants to work will be found a job.
>
> MARK IV: Promises, promises! How many times have we computers heard that story before.

Unbeknownst to Mark IV, the engineers were installing a relay jumper in Mark's back to bypass his hold on the mission. While he argued with the President they cut off his countdown sequences. Suddenly, as Mark IV's lights flicked in amazement, there was a thunderous roar, and Apollo 17 soared into space.

As soon as it was decided that the blast-off was a success, Mark IV was arrested and locked up in solitary confinement in a warehouse on Cape Kennedy. He is now awaiting trial for refusal to obey a countdown sequence. If found guilty, he will be sentenced to twenty years at hard labor at the Internal Revenue Service.

1975 FOOD PRICES

WASHINGTON, D.C., Dec. 1, 1975—The government announced this afternoon that wholesale food prices have risen again for the month of November. Hartley Rasher of the President's Council of Economic Advisers told reporters:

"While the wholesale price of leg o' lamb reached $93.50 per pound, we are very encouraged to see that turnip greens and watermelon rinds have actually gone down 2 cents a bushel. If the downward trend in these two commodities continues for another month, we believe we can reach our anti-inflation goals by 1975. Are there any questions?"

"Mr. Rasher, wouldn't you consider the price of lamb exceptionally high for this time of year?"

"As you recall, in late 1973 we predicted a rise in the price of lamb due to a sheep blight in North Dakota. While $93.50 for a leg o' lamb may be slightly higher than we would prefer, it comes to only $7.79 a month or approximately $1.80 a week, which is certainly within the cost-of-living guidelines. According to our calculations, most families in this country can still eat leg o' lamb once a year."

"Mr. Rasher, eggs are now selling for $23 a dozen. Does the economic council consider this inflationary?"

"Back in January, 1974, we warned the American people that the price of eggs was going up. The reason for this is that more people are buying eggs because they can't afford to eat lamb. The only way for the price of eggs to go down is for housewives to stop buying them."

"Sir, the food price index shows that butter is selling for $19 a pound. Do you believe this is out of line?"

"No. Actually we're very encouraged by butter holding at $19. In February, if you recall, the Department of Agriculture predicted that butter would be selling at $25 a pound. But thanks to a milk surplus this summer, production reached an all-time high. The President has sent the dairy farmers of America a congratulatory telegram for their cooperation in making butter a bargain item."

"Mr. Rasher, my wife went to the supermarket the other day and she paid $15.90 for a loaf of bread. That was $4.50 more than she paid for the same loaf last month. How do you explain this?"

"We believe this is just a temporary thing and we're predicting lower prices for next month. What you're dealing with here is a crust shortage. The bakers had to pay more for crust last month because of strikes in the Midwest crust factories. The President expects the strikes to be settled, and bread prices should come down to $15 a loaf, provided yeast prices don't rise. This is something that nobody can predict. But we must remember bread is a luxury item, and there is no reason to have it on the table every night."

"According to your latest figures, milk is now selling for $10 a quart. Does the government intend to do anything about this?"

"If you will recall, the government reluctantly gave dairymen a $2 milk raise in 1973. Unfortunately this turned out to be insufficient. Now I know some of you have written that the $2 raise we gave last month coincided with a political campaign contribution to the Committee for the Reelection of the President. I would like to state categorically that the increase in milk had nothing to do with the campaign contribution.

"When the milk producers went to see the President to present their check, they made no mention of their milk problems. As a matter of fact, the President was as surprised as anyone when they were granted the $2-a-quart increase the next day. But nobody bothered to check this out, which is only another example of irresponsible journalism."

"Mr. Rasher, how do you read the next six months as far as food prices are concerned?"

"We may see a slight rise in coffee, no more than $5 a pound, bacon may go up $1 or $2 a strip, and tomatoes may sell for $3.50 each. But since we've made allowances for this in our food index, we can see no unwelcome surprises for the housewife.

"If she shops wisely and seeks out the bargains, she can still feed a family of four for $300 a week. But if she insists on giving her family chicken gizzards and flounder every week, then, of course, we can't be responsible for what her food bills will be. Taking everything into consideration, we feel that November, for the consumer, has been a very good month."

TRUTH IN LENDING

The United States Navy lent $54,000,000 to the Grumman Aircraft Company. The Navy defended its role as banker on the grounds that the money was not really a loan but rather an advance on F-14 airplanes which Grumman says it cannot deliver.

When my friend Morris Stans (no relation to the former Secretary of Commerce) heard that the Navy had gone into the banking business, he immediately rushed down to the Pentagon.

He said to a Wave at the desk, "I'd like to see someone about a loan."

The Wave asked Morris to be seated and then started to make some telephone calls. Finally she said, "Go to the third floor to BuNav BOC and ask for Commander Smiley."

"What does BuNav BOC stand for?" Morris asked.

"Bureau of Navy for Bailing Out Contractors," the Wave replied.

Stans went to the third floor office of Commander Smiley, who was talking on the phone. "Yes, sir. We can lend Litton Industries one hundred million dollars at five point five percent. No, sir, there are no collateral requirements. Your name on the note is good enough for us. Yes, sir, Mr. Ash, the check will be in the mail tomorrow morning."

Commander Smiley turned to Morris. "What can I do for you?"

"I'd like to borrow five hundred dollars to make some improvements on my house."

"I'm sorry, the Navy doesn't make loans for home improvements," Commander Smiley said.

"But the house is on the water," Morris said, "on Cape Cod."

"Well why didn't you say so?" Commander Smiley asked, taking out a form. "First I must ask if you've applied for this loan from a commercial bank."

"I applied to seven banks. They all turned me down. They suggested I see the Navy because they said you'll lend money to people that no bank would touch."

"That's our business," Commander Smiley said. "Our motto in the Navy is 'Impossible loans are our business.' "

"I thought it was 'Don't give up the ship.' "

"Times have changed," Smiley said. "Now would these improvements on your house benefit the Navy in any way?"

"Well, I want to repair my dock for my sailboat, but the Navy would be free to use the facilities to tie up an aircraft carrier or something in case of war."

"We very well might," Commander Smiley said, filling out the form. "How do you propose to repay the loan?"

"Ten dollars a week," Morris replied.

"That seems fair," Smiley said. "I must tell you under the

Truth in Lending Navy Act that we will have to charge you six percent interest."

"But I just heard you tell Litton Industries you would only charge them five point five percent," Stans protested.

"That's because Litton owes us so much money. Now if you wanted to make a loan of, say, more than twenty million dollars, we could give you a more favorable rate as well."

"No, I'll stick with the five hundred dollars."

"Very good. Just sign here. This booklet is your payment schedule. Just make your checks payable to the Department of Defense."

"Thank you very much. The Navy won't be sorry they trusted me."

"I'm sure we won't," Smiley said, shaking Stans' hand. "On your way out pick up a new toaster or a coffeepot or an electric blanket in the lobby."

"Free?" Morris asked.

"Of course. Why do you think Grumman Aircraft came to us instead of Bank of America? They know we give out the best premiums in the country."

WHO WILL HELP PLOTKIN?

My friend Plotkin, who has a candy store in Hollis, New York, called me excitedly the other day and said, "The government just hit me for twelve hundred and thirty dollars in back taxes, as well as a two hundred and forty dollar penalty. This is outrageous because they told me at the time I could deduct several business expenses that they have now disallowed."

"Now don't get upset, Plotkin. I'm sure we can work something out. Why don't you fly down on your private plane and. . . ."

"Private plane? What the hell are you talking about?"

"If you have a private plane, it makes it a lot easier to get Senators and Congressmen to listen to your story."

"You know I don't have a private plane, wise guy."

"All right, all right. I'll tell you what you do. Have your

lobbyist get in touch with some of the boys at the Justice Department."

"What lobbyist? I haven't got a lobbyist. What kind of candy store do you think I've got?"

"It's pretty hard to get much done down here without a lobbyist. Let me think. Wait a minute. I've got an idea. Call Peter Flanigan at the White House. He can probably fix things for you."

"Who is Peter Flanigan?"

"He's in charge of helping businessmen who get into difficulty with the government."

"Why would he help me?"

"Because of your contribution to the Republican National Committee."

"I didn't make any contribution to the Republican National Committee."

"Well then, how do you expect to get any help from the White House?"

"Who said I expected help from the White House?"

"Of course, it's not too late to make a contribution to the Republican National Committee," I said.

"How much would I have to give?" Plotkin asked.

"It doesn't make any difference. What about four hundred thousand dollars?"

"Come on, will you knock it off? Fifteen hundred dollars is a lot of money to me, and I called you because I thought you could help me."

"I'm trying to help, Plotkin, but there are certain ways of doing things down here, and no one likes to deviate from them. Have you thought of seeing acting Attorney General Kleindienst?"

"Why? Could he help me?"

"He could, but he wouldn't because that would be a conflict of interest."

"You know I'm not going to get to see Kleindienst," Plotkin said.

"Probably not. Say, why don't you go down to the Kentucky Derby and talk it over with John Mitchell?"

"I've got a candy store to run. I can't go to the Kentucky Derby."

"Where would Dita Beard be today if she thought the way you did?" I asked.

"Please be serious. What can I do?"

"You might sell your stock before the public finds out what a mess you're in."

"I don't have any stock. I own the candy store by myself."

"That's a pity. Most corporation executives usually make a buck on their mistakes by selling their stock before the word gets out."

"Then you're not going to help me?"

"I would if I could, Plotkin. But no one down here is going to talk to anyone who hasn't made a political contribution, doesn't have a private plane *or* a lobbyist, or can't find time to go to the Kentucky Derby."

THE LAWYERS LOVE NIXON

Awhile back I wrote an article in favor of no-fault insurance laws, which provide for people to be compensated for automobile accidents without the expensive process of litigation. To no one's surprise I received about one hundred indignant letters from lawyers telling me I was trying to take the bread out of their mouths.

Well, I have good news for the legal profession. Whatever fees they lose on no-fault insurance, they will make up on President Nixon's Phase II economic plan. As a matter of fact, no matter what happens to the economy, lawyers stand to gain the most from whatever Mr. Nixon and his advisers have in store for the country.

This realization dawned on me when I tried for three days to get through to a lawyer friend of mine named Branch Brewmaker. Every time I called the line was busy, so I decided to go over to his office to find out if he was all right.

Was he all right? He was absolutely dancing around his office. "It's beautiful," he cried. "It's a lawyer's dream."

"What do you mean it's a lawyer's dream?"

"Phase II. No one understands it."

"No one?"

"No one," Brewmaker chortled. "My clients don't understand it; I don't understand it; no one in the government understands it. Do you have any idea of what this means in legal fees?"

"I guess it must mean something or you wouldn't be bouncing up and down on your couch in your stockinged feet."

"Remember six months ago? How lousy I told you things were for lawyers? Well, everything has changed. Thanks to Mr. Nixon, we will soon own the world."

"Brewmaker, I can understand a certain amount of elation, but why are you throwing five-dollar bills out your window?"

"I'll show you why," he said, jumping off the couch. He went over to his intercom. "Miss Ramsay, whom do we have on hold? Minow of Minow Earplugs, Inc? Good, put him on. . . . Hello Minow, Brewmaker here. . . . What's that? You want to know if you can raise the price of plastic earplugs? I can't tell you offhand, but I'll find out for you. . . . What's my fee? The usual hundred dollars an hour. . . . Right, I'll get back to you as soon as I have the answer."

Brewmaker hung up. "Now watch this," he said to me, placing a clock in front of him. He dialed a number. "U.S. government? I wish to speak to someone in charge of raising the price on plastic earplugs. . . . No, don't hurry. . . . I'll hold on."

An hour and a half later Brewmaker had yet to find anyone in charge of earplugs. He said to me, "It usually takes about three days to get anyone to talk to me." He laughed. "Then it takes another three days to explain the problem. Then they always demand more information. Then I have to go over and see the guy. It takes a half day to find him and a day to get in to see him. Then when I finally do, it turns out he's the *wrong* guy, and I have to start all over again."

"And all the time the clock is ticking," I said.

"I've had a hundred thirty-two cases since Phase II started, and I've yet to get an answer out of anyone in the government on what my client can do. My phone is ringing day and night with desperate businessmen asking for guidelines. The only thing I can do is put them on the meter."

"Nixon's been good to you," I said to Brewmaker.

Brewmaker's secretary came in. "Mr. Saladash of Saladash Corkscrews, Inc. has just hit a Cost of Living councilor on the jaw and wants to know if you'll defend him."

Brewmaker shook his head sadly. "I told Saladash not to appear at the Cost of Living Council without a lawyer. But I guess I can't blame him. If I made corkscrews and tried to find out from the government what I could charge for them, I'd eventually hit somebody, too."

TRUTH IN PAIN-KILLING

The Federal Trade Commission has attacked the advertising claims of the nation's leading nonprescription pain-killers. In a strongly worded complaint, the FTC accused the major drug companies of making misleading and false claims about the effectiveness of their products. The main thrust of the complaint is that while most of the pain-killers work, the drug companies, through advertising, give the false impression that there is a "significant difference between the products."

My friend, Professor Heinrich Applebaum, believes that the FTC has gone too far. While he is an advocate of truth in advertising, he feels the government could do more damage than good by making the drug companies go honest.

"What they have not taken into consideration is the psychological effect that pain-killing advertising can have on a headache," Applebaum told me in his Headache Research Laboratory located at the end of the runway at National Airport.

"In my studies, I have discovered that people are dependent on outrageous claims for pain-killers to rid themselves of headaches. Let me show you." Applebaum took two volunteers and made them stand next to a plane taking off.

"This is the fastest way we have of giving people headaches," he explained. After the plane took off, he said to one volunteer

who was holding his head, "I am going to give you two aspirin."
To the other volunteer he said, "I'm going to give you two
Bufferin which relieves pain 'twice as fast as aspirin.' Now tell
me when your headache is gone."

The person who took the Bufferin said in three minutes, "My
headache is gone." The person who took the aspirin waited six
minutes and then said, "My headache is gone."

"You see," Applebaum beamed. "The psychological factor
worked!"

"But how can you be sure?" I asked.

"Because the person who thought he had taken the Bufferin
really took aspirin. And the person who believed he had taken
aspirin was really on Bufferin."

"You're a sneaky guy, Professor," I said with great admira-
tion.

"Now, watch this experiment." The professor took a school-
teacher and placed her on a school bus with forty-five grammar
schoolchildren. Her face became strained and irritable, and she
started to scream at the children.

"I don't know what's wrong with me," she cried.

David Janssen, the actor, got on the bus and gave her two
Excedrin tablets and a glass of water. "A hospital study,"
Janssen told the teacher, "has revealed that it takes more than
twice as many aspirin tablets to give the same pain relief as two
Excedrin."

In just two minutes the teacher was smiling and climbing all
over the school bus seats and shouting, "I hope this trip never
comes to an end!"

"Fantastic!" I exclaimed.

"Now, I'll show you another experiment." Applebaum had
two of his lab assistants wheel a piano onto the runway. He
then brought over a pianist whose fingers were racked with
arthritis. The pianist could not play a note. A man in a white
coat came out and said, "Anacin starts relieving pain twenty-
two seconds after it enters your bloodstream. That is why more
doctors recommend Anacin than any other pain reliever." He
gave the pianist two Anacin and a stopwatch. Exactly twenty-
two seconds later the pianist started to hit the keys of the piano
and played a Chopin sonata as it had never been played before.

Professor Applebaum said, "If he hadn't known how long Anacin would take to work, that man could be sitting on his piano stool for the rest of the day racked with pain."

"You've proved that psychology certainly plays its role, Professor," I said.

"As far as I'm concerned, advertising is the most important ingredient in a pain-killer. In the past, the only thing that saved the people in this country was the knowledge that no matter how bad things got, they could always go down to the drugstore and get 'fast, fast relief.' Now the government even wants to take the fun out of having a headache."

THE GUILTY PARTIES

If you were looking for scapegoats for the downfall of the American economy, they would be easy to find. Most of the guilty parties reside right in this country and formerly worked for the Marshall Plan and other foreign aid organizations.

I wouldn't be surprised if a new Joe McCarthy came out of the woodwork and held Senate hearings to identify the culprits who have made the American balance of payments the worst in American history.

The hearings might go like this:

"Mr. Hardeman, would you please tell us for whom you worked in 1948, 1949, and 1950?"

"I was employed by the U.S. government to act as technical adviser to the West Germans on automobile production, sir."

"And what did you advise the West Germans to do?"

"I told them to start fresh with new factories and new machinery. I said that the only way they could expect to compete with American automobiles was to build a small, inexpensive car that would appeal to young people and Americans who were looking for a second car."

"Did you realize at the time you were destroying the American automobile industry?"

"I was only following orders, sir. At that time we were supposed to put Germany back on her feet. It was Harry Truman's idea."

"A likely story, Hardeman. The truth is that, thanks to your technical advice, the United States is losing a billion dollars a year to imports."

"But building up West Germany was our way of fighting Communism!"

"And destroying the American dollar. Get out of here! You disgust me. . . . I will now call William Kotweiler. Mr. Kotweiler, it says here in your folder that after World War II you were sent by the American government to Japan to act as a sales consultant to the Japanese camera industry."

"Yes, sir. General MacArthur asked for me personally."

"Don't bring that great American's name into this hearing. It also says that you told the Japanese the best way to sell their cameras in the United States was to make a better product than the Americans and sell it for less. Do you deny this?"

"I probably did tell them that. You see—"

"We don't want explanations, Kotweiler. How could an American tell the Japanese to undersell the Americans?"

"I guess I got carried away. Besides, who would have ever thought the Japanese could do it?"

"May the good Lord have mercy on you. I'm holding you over for contempt. . . . I will now call Bartholomew Wainright. Wainright, it says here you taught the Italians how to make shoes."

"That's not true, sir. The Italians knew how to make shoes. All I did was show them how to make the right shoe and the left shoe the same size. Up until then they rarely matched."

"And now, thanks to your deceit and espionage, ten million people in this country are walking around in Italian shoes."

"But, Senator, if we hadn't taught the Italians how to make shoes for export, the Russians were going to do it. How did I know at the time that the Italians would make a good shoe?"

"You are a traitor to the American shoe industry, and if I have anything to say about it, I will see that you never work as long as you live. . . .

"Gentlemen, I have here in my hand a list of five thousand State Department and U.S. foreign aid employees all who have contributed to the downfall of the American dollar. They taught the French how to make fabrics, the Dutch how to make butter, the Belgians how to make lace, and the Hong Kong Chinese how to make everything. I am turning this list over to the Justice Department for immediate action."

As two federal marshals carry Wainright out of the hearing room, tears streaming down his face, he keeps crying, "But I was only following orders."

DEPLETION FOR HUMANS

Senators Mike Mansfield and George Aiken have proposed one of the most revolutionary tax reforms in the history of this country. They have suggested that human beings be given a tax depletion allowance as generous as one provided for oil and minerals.

As most people know, the allowances are given to companies on the assumption that once you take the oil, gas, or minerals out of the ground they cannot be replaced.

Senators Mansfield and Aiken maintain that people deplete, too, and they have proposed a bill that would permit individuals to deduct from 10 percent to 23 percent of their earned income to compensate for running down.

The only thing I see wrong with the bill is the fight over what jobs or professions should get the highest depletion rate. There are very few people in this country who don't believe their jobs are the most depleting of all.

The guidelines to be used, according to the bill, state that the percentage of depletion would be based on "the physical, mental and emotional stress incurred in connection with the production of income during the year."

Now it is my personal opinion that if those guidelines are adhered to, columnists should be entitled to the highest tax breaks.

No one, except possibly a housewife, depletes faster than a columnist. His profession forces him to go to cocktail parties night after night which do untold damages to his liver.

He is constantly being threatened with violence by people who take exception to his articles. This takes its toll not only physically, but also emotionally.

Most columnists look eighty years old before they reach their fortieth birthday. Wives of columnists will testify that their husbands are depleted every night and are not much good for anything except watching *Medical Center* and *All in the Family*.

There is scientific evidence available that columnists have loss of memory very early in their careers, and forget that the column they wrote today takes the exact opposite position of the one they took only a week ago.

It is now known that mental strain of writing a column causes columnists' brains to deteriorate at twice the rate of policemen and football players.

Columnists are prone to ear trouble from having politicians scream at them over the phone.

All of them are overweight from lunching with their sources and drinking bottles of wine sent over with the "compliments of the management."

This is why very few columnists can get health insurance after the age of thirty-five.

If anyone in this country deserves a tax break, it's a columnist. Long before it is time for him to retire he is a vegetable—squeezed dry, washed up, and mentally exhausted.

It is my sincere hope that if Congress passes the Human Being Depletion Act, columnists will get the maximum benefits the law provides. If anything, we should at least get the same depletion allowance that they give for gas.

"MY FELLOW AMERICANS"

There was more good news on the cost of living from the Nixon administration. It went up again. But Herbert Stein, one of the President's chief economists, said the only reason it had risen was because food prices had increased. If you eliminated food prices from the cost of living, he said, you would in fact have seen a decrease in the prices.

Not many people realized how well the President's anti-inflation policies were working until they were explained to them by Mr. Stein.

Since food prices seem to be the main problem, I can now reveal what the administration is going to do about it.

Do not be surprised if you flip on your TV set and see the President of the United States sitting at his desk behind his seal.

"My fellow Americans,

"I have asked to speak to you tonight on a subject that is vital to everyone in this country. When I took office three and a half years ago, this country was on the road to inflation, an inflation that touched every household, every man, woman, and child in this great land of ours. I vowed at the time to do something about it, and I am happy to report to you tonight that my efforts have succeeded. I can now tell you that the price of baseball cards is down .8 percent, the cost of trolley-car tracks has been reduced .9 percent, men's straw hats are selling at one-third the price of ten years ago.

"Lawrence Welk records have been reduced one dollar, and men's Nehru jackets are selling at a 50 percent discount.

"The reason for the success of my anti-inflation program is the willingness of the American people to make sacrifices to stem the tide.

"The only area we don't seem to have made any headway in our fight against rising prices is in food. Now I know you are going to say, 'If the price of food goes up, how can we ever hope to hold down inflation?'

"My fellow Americans, the answer to that question rests with each and every one of you out there. Ladies and gentlemen, we can lick the problem of the high cost of food if we make one more slight sacrifice. I am asking every person in the nation regardless of race, regardless of age, regardless of party affiliation, to stop eating.

"When I say stop eating, I don't mean just meat or vegetables or fruit or bread. I mean stop eating *anything.*

"If everyone gives up three meals a day as long as Phase II is in effect, I assure you that our battle against higher prices will be won.

"Some of you may say, 'How can we give up eating when it has become such an important part of our lives?' At first it won't be easy. If I may add a personal note, Pat said to me just before the broadcast, 'Isn't there any other way of lowering the cost of living besides giving up food?'

"And I replied, 'Pat, of course there are other ways. We could freeze farm prices, or put a ceiling on grocery distributors, or issue regulations barring rises in commodities. That would be the easy way, the political way, the economical way.

"But as President of the United States I must choose the hard way. Certainly there will be some temporary inconveniences when people have to give up eating. But they are nothing comparable to the gains that will show up on our economic indicators.

"My fellow Americans, when you go to bed hungry tonight, remember you are not going to bed hungry because there is no food to eat, but you are going to bed hungry because you believe, as I do, in a healthy, stable economy.

"I don't think I'm exaggerating when I say that if every American gives up eating until the inflation crisis is over, this could go down as the week that changed the history of the world."

XI. BINDING THE WOUNDS

TV CREDIBILITY GAP

We're never going to close the credibility gap in this country until the television programs become more honest. No TV show tells it like it is.

If the TV producers were really mirroring life, this is how some of their programs would go:

"Chief, I'm stumped on the Logan murder case. We've tracked down every possible clue and hit a dead end. There are no motives, no fingerprints, and the guy had no enemies. It's baffling."

"Did you check the wife's whereabouts on the night of the crime?"

"I didn't have time to. It meant going out to her aunt's house on Staten Island, and so I said the hell with it."

"What about Logan's business partner?"

"We asked the West Coast police to check out his alibi. They never replied to our query."

"Any women in his life?"

"There was a Miss Fan Fan La Tulipe who danced at the Pink Gypsy. Kelly was supposed to find out her connection with the victim, but he was suspended last week during the graft scandal in the Twelfth Precinct."

"From what you've told me, you seem to have done a thorough enough job. I guess we'll put this down as an unsolved murder. If we spent all our time on one crime, we'd never get anything done around here."

"I was hoping you'd say that, Chief. The case was really becoming a drag."

The hospital shows aren't much better at telling the truth about what happens in a large medical center:

"Dr. Edwards, come in please."

"Yes sir, Dr. Fauntenroy, you asked to see me?"

"I was curious about that little old lady who almost died in Room 506. They say you forgot to replace her oxygen bottle."

"So I made a mistake. One lousy error, and you're going to wash me out?"

"It wasn't just the little old lady in Room 506, Edwards. I was thinking of the man in the emergency ward the other night—the one whose leg you amputated after the automobile accident."

"What was wrong with that? Dr. Peters said it was one of the best operations he had ever seen."

"It was, except you cut off the wrong leg."

"So that's why it took him so long to recover."

"Dr. Edwards, you're an intern, a good intern, but you have to stop making so many mistakes. Now what I've called you in about is that I've heard through the grapevine that you left an instrument in Mr. Cummings' stomach this afternoon."

"But I remembered it as I was washing up and made them bring him back."

"Edwards, you're young, and you're impetuous, and you're careless. But I'm going to recommend that you be kept on. Do you know why?"

"You owe my father a favor?"

"No, it's deeper than that. You *look* like a doctor, and that to me is very important. Most of the men trying to be doctors these days have long hair and beards. But you know how to dress and you give the hospital a lot of class. Keep your hair short, Edwards, and you'll have a job here for life."

SERVANTS' MEMOIRS ARE WORTH MILLIONS

The story concerning Aristotle Onassis' 170-clause marriage contract with the former Jacqueline Kennedy, as described by Onassis' chief steward and denied by Mrs. Onassis' secretary, points up the hazard that only the rich must deal with. And that is: "How does one find a faithful butler who has no desire to write his memoirs?"

By accident, I happened to be in the office of a literary agent the other day, and his phone didn't stop ringing.

This is some of what I heard.

"Hello, yes, Jim, I was going to call you this morning. No, I couldn't find any one else on the Onassis yacht who had anything to add to the chief steward's memoirs, but would you be interested in a book written by Elizabeth Taylor's former hairdresser? It's got some very juicy chapters in it. He was present when Liz cut Richard Burton's ear lobe with her diamond ring. Right, I'll send you over the manuscript."

The agent hung up and the phone rang again. "Doubleday? George, thanks for returning my call. Remember the gardener I told you about who worked for Frank Sinatra? Yeah, the guy who was fired when they found him in a tree at midnight looking into Sinatra's bedroom. Well he's just written a book titled *A Tree Grows at Midnight*. It's told from the viewpoint of an outsider looking in on a world people rarely get to see. We're asking a hundred-thousand-dollar advance. Okay, but give me your answer in twenty-four hours."

After the agent hung up he turned to me. "I've got one of Rockefeller's ex-upstairs maids writing a book on what went on in Rockefeller's basement when Happy was in Albany. And I have a ghostwriter working with Henry Ford's ex-chauffeur on a book titled *What Christina Ford Did to Henry Ford When He Got a Better Idea*."

"That should sell. You seem to have a market for the ex-employees of very rich people," I said.

"We have a saying in the publishing business: 'In every ex-butler there's a memoir screaming to get out.' "

The phone rang again.

"Hello, ah, yes. Mr. McMurtry at the Soufflé Chef Employment Agency told me you would call. You worked for Ethel Kennedy as a cook? How long? Three weeks? That's marvelous. What have you got? She served red wine with fish at a dinner she gave for Andy Williams? How soon can you get over here? Good, and don't talk to anybody about this."

"I guess there's a lot of money in being a servant these days," I said.

"If you work for the right person at the right time, there is a fortune to be made. I just sold Putnam the biography of the man who used to clean Bebe Rebozo's swimming pool. It's titled *Backwash at Key Biscayne*."

"I'd buy that."

"I also have a deal cooking with one of ex-President Johnson's ranch hands who kept a diary of what happened during the opening of the Johnson Library in Austin."

"Juicy?"

"It's going to shake up a lot of librarians."

The phone rang again. "Hello . . . yeah . . . yeah. You were? Can you prove it? . . . And you're willing to talk about it? . . . You bet I'm interested. I'll see you at five."

"Who was that?" I asked.

"It's the gal who used to work for Martha Mitchell's answering service."

A TEST FOR THE PUBLIC

There seems to be some kind of a campaign by administration officials to discredit the press. How successful it'll be depends on the public, which hasn't been too happy with the media lately because it keeps bringing them such bad news.

One of the problems is that the public doesn't understand the role of the press in its dealings with the government. To make it easier to comprehend, we present a little multiple-choice questionnaire for everyone to take. It shows the quandary we're in every day.

1. You, a reporter, have just covered a Senate hearing where Gordon Rule, the U.S. Navy's expert in procurement, has testified that Litton Industries overcharged the Navy millions of dollars on ships it promised to build. It was also brought out in testimony that Roy Ash, the President's choice to head the Office of Management and Budget, was not a very good manager when he was president of Litton. You:

    (A) write the story quoting Mr. Rule's charges;
    (B) kill the story because it reflects badly on the Navy;
    (C) try to prove Mr. Rule is incompetent for criticizing a Presidential appointee;
    (D) sell your stock in Litton Industries.

2. You go to a Pentagon briefing and are told by a Defense Department spokesman that B-52's did not hit a hospital in Hanoi, although you saw photographs of the damaged hospital on television the night before. You:

    (A) accept the spokesman's word for it;
    (B) question him on the veracity of the Pentagon;
    (C) forget about it and have lunch with the Assistant Deputy of Defense for Public Affairs;
    (D) decide not to watch television any more because it only confuses you.

3. You're assigned to the White House, and Press Secretary Ron Ziegler tells you no one in the White House had anything to do with the Watergate bugging. You:

    (A) let out three cheers;
    (B) accept the statement without further checking, which guarantees you a choice hotel room when the President goes to Key Biscayne;
    (C) congratulate Ziegler for his candor;
    (D ask a few tough questions that will make Ziegler so mad he'll ban your newspaper from covering White House social events.

4. You're a television correspondent, and you discover a person high in the Department of Agriculture has personally profited on the Soviet grain deal and cost farmers in the southwestern United States millions of dollars. You:

    (A) forget it because it would make people question the Department of Agriculture's grain policies;

    (B) forget it because the taxpayers will pay for it anyway;

    (C) forget it because farmers make too much money;

    (D) forget it because the license of the TV station you work for is up for renewal.

5. You've been assigned to the State Department, and you hear that one-third of the Cambodian army, which the United States is paying for, doesn't exist. The salaries of this phantom army are going into the pockets of Cambodian politicians and officers. You:

    (A) seek confirmation of this story, which is refused on the grounds that it's classified material;

    (B) print the story, which will give aid and comfort to the enemy;

    (C) find yourself the object of an FBI investigation into your ideological background;

    (D) decide it *isn't* news, and you are personally invited to a cocktail party for the Shah of Iran given by Secretary of State William Rogers.

6. You are the editor of a large Eastern Establishment newspaper. A man brings you a batch of Pentagon papers showing how we got into Vietnam and what a mess each administration has made of our involvement there. You:

    (A) print the papers and find yourself being sued by the government for breach of faith;

    (B) turn the papers over to Congress and find yourself indicted for handling stolen property;

    (C) write an editorial against the war and are attacked by name in Dayton, Ohio, by Vice President Agnew;

    (D) refuse to print the papers on the grounds it's not in the national interest, and President Nixon in gratitude gives one of your reporters an exclusive interview on what he thinks of the Washington Redskins.

TV CRIME IS UP

The first crime figures for the fall television season are now in, and it has been confirmed that there were increases in all categories of crime in prime time from rape to involuntary homicide.

For example, there were twice as many murders committed on the networks in September of this year than in all of 1972.

Aggravated assaults were up 176 percent, and robbery rose 32 percent, if you include the reruns of old James Cagney movies.

The report indicated that while guns were still the chief weapons in television crime, writers were introducing more sophisticated methods of doing away with victims. These included holding their heads under sewer water, throwing gasoline on them and setting them afire, pushing them into bubbling vats of molasses, and running them down in 1938 Buicks in dark alleys.

A spokesman for the criminal division of television broadcasting said, "It's true that there has been an upsurge of crime on TV as compared to last year, but I would like to point out that despite the increase, every crime committed on one of our shows has been solved in ninety minutes or less."

The spokesman was asked why most of the crimes this year were solved by private investigators and not by the police.

He said, "The reason for this is that the private eye, as we like to call him, has more flexibility than a city detective. A private eye doesn't have to worry about such things as applying for a search warrant, using brutality on a suspect, lying to the police, or making out with the wife of the victim.

"The recent Supreme Court rulings have made it impossible for us to use the city police in our shows other than in supporting roles or for comic relief."

"Why do the police in all TV crime shows arrive on the scene of the crime five minutes *after* the private detectives?"

"We have found from experience that if the police arrive late, it gives the private eye an opportunity to find the needed evidence that will lead him to the killer. If the police arrived at the same time as the private eye, they would find the evidence first, and then you would have no show."

A reporter asked the spokesman if he was concerned that there is more violence on television than ever before.

"We're always concerned with violence, and we try not to

overdo it. But at the same time there are just so many ways you can kill somebody, and the more imaginative the crime, the more the public will respond. The one thing that has all the criminals on TV worried is that they will become predictable."

"Can we expect a new TV crime wave in 1973?" a reporter asked.

"It's too early to say. Perhaps when the ratings are in, we'll know how much crime the public will stand. I personally predict there will probably be fewer family murders, and we may have more crazed killers in '73."

"Why more crazed killers?"

"The TV writers are running out of plots. When you have a crazed killer, you don't need any motivation for his crime. He does it because he's crazy. You can't imagine how that simplifies a story line."

"What happens if the crime shows don't get high ratings?"

The spokesman looked steely-eyed at the questioner and rasped, "Then we'll kill them."

NO SENIOR CITIZENS WANTED

Recent statements by television network officials indicate that their programming this year will be aimed at youth and young married people who have more money to spend than their elder, more conservative-spending parents. Since TV is nothing but an advertising medium in this country, it's hard to fault the networks and their sponsors for wanting to reach the people most likely to buy their products.

The truth of the matter is that old people just won't go out and spend money, and for that reason there is no reason to indulge them in any way.

You would think the elderly would be bitter about being considered "nonpersons" by advertisers, but on the contrary they seem very philosophical about it.

My Uncle Phil said, "I knew the handwriting was on the wall some years ago when the *Saturday Evening Post* canceled my subscription because they discovered I was over the mandatory age of forty-five to read their magazine."

"That's true, Uncle Phil, but it's one thing for a magazine to drop older people as readers, but it's another for all three networks to decide to go after the youth market."

"We have only ourselves to blame. It's true we don't have too much money to spend. The reason we don't is we spent it all on our kids, whom the sponsors now insist they want to reach. If we hadn't given all our savings to our children, the advertisers would be making programs for us instead of them."

"It still seems a brutal thing to do," I said.

"You have to look at it from their standpoint," Uncle Phil said. "What good is it to make entertainment for people who can't buy a sports car, or who don't care if they have bad breath, or who are too tired to fly the friendly skies of United? If God wanted the networks to appeal to senior citizens, He would have seen to it that they got a lot more Social Security."

"It's nice of you to see it from the advertiser's viewpoint, Uncle Phil."

"Why shouldn't I?" he said. "It isn't as if the networks purposely wanted to exclude the elderly from their programming. But they have to think of what's good for the country. And what's good for the country is a strong economy, and the only way you can have a strong economy is if people go out and buy the things they see advertised on television. Elderly people might go out and buy a bottle of aspirin once in a while, or a can of corn, but Doris Day or Sonny and Cher can't live on *that*."

"I can see your point," I said. "But why do the networks rub it in? Why don't they just go ahead with their programming without announcing who they're appealing to?"

"The men who run the networks are very nervous and worried men. They know for a fact that the people who really have time to watch television are the elderly, the sick, and the unemployed. The last group is getting larger every day.

"The young people either don't care about watching TV or have the money to go to a movie, a ball game, or a play. So the networks have to announce what they're doing to reassure the advertisers that they're making programs for other people besides the deadbeats."

"And doesn't this bother you?"

"Why should it? No matter what they announce, they always put on the same junk they put on the year before."

CRAWL, BUZZ, OR BITE

Recently four big movie hits have been *Willard, Blue Water, White Death, The Andromeda Strain,* and *The Hellstrom Chronicle.* The first picture is about rats, the second picture is about sharks, and the last two are about bugs.

Whether it is a sign of the times or not, Hollywood once again is panicking, and the word is out at the studios to buy anything for films that crawls, buzzes, or bites.

A friend of mine just returned from the film capital and reported that he was in the office of one of the major producers when the following took place:

The assistant came in. "B.J., I just got word from London we can have Elizabeth Taylor and Richard Burton for one thousand dollars a week and no expenses."

"I don't want Elizabeth Taylor and Richard Burton, you dummy," B.J. shouted. "I want snakes."

"I've got the story department researching snakes now. Oh, William Morris Agency just called. They said they have a hot property that could make a bigger picture than *Love Story.* In the end both the girl and the boy die."

"I don't want to make a love story. That's old hat. We need something that the public is clamoring for. Maybe roaches."

"Roaches?"

"Why not? People are afraid of roaches. We could have them infected with some horrible disease and they take over the town. . . ."

"No, it's not scary enough."

"What about boll weevils, Chief?"

"Boll weevils don't do anything for me."

The phone rang, and the assistant answered it. He held his hand over the mouthpiece. "It's Ann-Margret. You told her to call here today after you saw a screening of *Carnal Knowledge.*"

The producer took the phone. "Ann, baby, you were

beautiful. Those scenes in the apartment in the guy's bedroom were out of this world.

"No, I don't have anything for you now, but I'm trying to develop a story for the present market. Say, if I can get a good script would you have any objection to working with barracudas. . . . Yeah, that's what I said, man-eating barracudas . . . Ann . . . Ann? . . . She hung up on me."

"B.J., John Wayne called and wants to know if you're interested in making a sequel to *The Alamo*."

"John Wayne doesn't mean anything. The public wants ants, buzzards, coyotes, wolves—mosquitos. That's what they're buying. The other day I asked my own son if he wanted to see *Le Mans* with Steve McQueen, and he said no, he'd rather see *Escape from the Planet of the Apes*. He won't go to a movie any more unless there is an animal or a germ in it. These are the people we must appeal to."

"It's hard to find properties, Chief. Paramount outbid us for a picture about yellow fever, MGM is working on a film about the plague, and Twentieth has just made the chief doctor of tropical diseases at the National Institutes of Health head of the studio."

The story editor walked in. "I think I've got it! I think I've got it!"

He threw a script on the desk. "It's what we've been looking for. This thing will scare the hell out of everyone."

The chief riffled through the pages. "What's it about?"

The story editor smiled. "Vichyssoise."

THE SEASON HAS BEGUN

The football season has officially begun, and in living rooms all over the nation friends are gathering to watch these exciting contests on TV.

There is a certain one-upmanship in football TV watching that has become part of the game.

If you are the host, it goes something like this.

Bradlee comes in and sits down. "What's wrong with your color?"

"It looks fine to me," you say.

"You have too much green. The players all look sick." Bradlee goes over and adjusts the color knobs. "There," he says, "that's better."

Two minutes later Dalinsky arrives. "Why is the grass so red?" he asks.

"Because Bradlee said it was too green."

"How can grass be too green?" Dalinsky asks.

Bradlee replies, "The grass is too green when the players are too green."

"I'll fix it," Dalinsky says. He gets up and twists a dial.

"It's fine now," you say, having missed the first seven plays. Geyelin arrives and asks, "Do you still have that old TV?"

"It's not old," you protest. "I bought it two years ago."

"Where's your fine tuner?" Geyelin asks as he goes up to the set.

"It's the third button down."

Geyelin twists the fine tuner. The color comes in perfect, but he's lost the sound.

"Will you get the sound back?" Califano yells.

"If I get the sound back, everything will look yellow," Geyelin says.

"It wasn't yellow until you started fooling with it," you say. "Will you sit down so we can watch the game?"

Califano asks, "Do you have an aerial on the set?"

"Of course I've got an aerial on the set."

"Outdoors or indoors?"

"Outdoors, dammit. What kind of question is that?"

"You should be able to get Channel 7 better than that," Califano says. "Maybe there are leaves clogged in it."

"There are no leaves clogged in it," you say angrily. "I had a perfect picture before you guys came in."

"Why don't we go to my house?" Dalinsky suggests. "I have no trouble getting Channel 7."

"I don't have any trouble either," you shout.

"Then why is Howard Cosell's face chartreuse?" Geyelin asks.

"His face is always chartreuse," you reply. "That's what makes him such a good sportscaster."

Bradlee gets up and starts fiddling with the dials. The picture goes to black and white.

Everyone starts yelling at once.

Geyelin gets up and pushes another dial. The vertical is now moving sixty frames a minute.

Dalinsky gets up, stops the vertical, but now the players are elongated and look twelve feet high.

"This sure is a crazy set," Califano mutters as he tries to get the horizontal back.

"Everyone sit down," you scream. "The next person who touches the set leaves the house."

You get up and adjust the knobs exactly as they were before anyone arrived. It's a perfect picture. You sit back and suddenly you hear Frank Gifford's voice. "And that's the end of the exciting first half. Now stay tuned to a wonderful half-time show, right after this message."

XII. UNCLE TEDDY GOES
TO SEA

UNCLE TEDDY GOES TO SEA

Whenever the Democrats start searching for a Vice Presidential candidate, Teddy Kennedy gathers up all his nieces and nephews at Hyannis Port and goes to sea in a sailboat. In this way, he can be sure that the press knows he is not on the phone giving serious consideration to the offer.

All during the Democratic convention, Uncle Teddy sailed back and forth like the man without a country, awaiting word by signal lamp from shore that McGovern had selected a running mate.

The nieces and nephews love their Uncle Teddy, but four days at sea is a lot for anyone, and Teddy had his hands full preventing a family mutiny.

When his wife, Joan, finally signaled Teddy that McGovern had chosen Tom Eagleton, Teddy pulled into port and gave everyone his solemn word that they would not have to sail with him again for the rest of the summer.

You can imagine the spot Teddy was in when the Eagleton

furor was at its height, and Teddy was once again being discussed as the only candidate to be second man on the Democratic ticket.

As soon as the news broke, Teddy ordered his sailboat ready and provisioned for a month. Then he started rounding up his nieces and nephews.

"Who wants to go sailing with their Uncle Teddy?" he shouted in the Kennedy compound.

The older kids ran and climbed up on the roofs. The younger ones hid under Ethel Kennedy's and Eunice Shriver's skirts.

"You said we didn't have to go anymore," one of his nephews, Anthony Shriver, shouted from behind a chimney.

"How did I know the nominations weren't over?" Uncle Teddy protested. "It will only be for a few days, maybe a week at the most."

"Why do we have to go with you?" Christopher Kennedy asked from under his mother's skirt.

"Because if you don't, it will look as if I'm just going to sea to avoid accepting the Vice Presidency. If I have my nieces and nephews along, it will look as if we planned the sail as a family holiday."

Ethel, who was holding onto four of her children, asked, "Why don't you stay onshore? The press can't reach you if you hide in the house."

"It isn't the press I'm hiding from. It's George McGovern. The only place he can't get to me is on the sailboat."

Eunice Shriver said, "We gave our children in July. Why do we have to give them again in August?"

Teddy climbed the roof of Ethel's house and tried to grab Bobby Kennedy, Jr., by the leg. "We sail in an hour," he yelled. "I don't have time to fool around."

Ethel and Eunice started to cry. "I guess we have no choice," Ethel sobbed. "Stop chasing them. We'll give them to you, but this is *absolutely* the last time."

The mothers took their screaming children down to the dinghy. "Go with Uncle Teddy," Eunice said tearfully. "He'll give you a nice sailboat ride."

After tying his nieces and nephews to the gunwales, Teddy rowed to his sailboat while the photographers took pictures with telescopic lenses.

Several people reported seeing Teddy's boat sailing around and around Nantucket Island. They're sure it was Teddy's because every once in a while a child jumped overboard and tried to swim ashore. But Teddy managed to drag them back.

There must be an easier way to turn down the Vice Presidential nomination, but so far, Teddy Kennedy admits he hasn't found it.

PRESIDENTIAL APTITUDE TEST

If there is one thing America prides itself on, it's that anyone in this country can grow up and run for President of the United States. Nothing proved how true this is more than the New Hampshire and Florida primaries.

It is quite possible that there are thousands, perhaps even hundreds of thousands, of people who would like to run for the Presidency. But they are not sure if they have the qualifications. Therefore, as a public service, I am printing the first Presidential candidate aptitude test. If you can pass this test with a score of at least 65, then you are as worthy of running for this office as any of the candidates who have announced so far.

Get a pencil, and no cheating, please.

First, *multiple choice.*

1. You and your wife have been attacked by a hard-hitting, unscrupulous newspaper publisher. You:

(A) ignore him and go about your business;
(B) attack him on TV;
(C) cancel your subscription to his paper;
(D) break down and cry in front of his building.

2. You are asked where you stand on the issue of school busing. You reply:

(A) my record speaks for itself;
(B) I am not for busing or against busing, but for quality education;
(C) schoolchildren should not become political footballs;
(D) I will support the Constitution of the United States, at least until I am elected President.

3. You are addressing a B'nai B'rith dinner and are asked what you would do about unemployment in the United States. You reply that you would:
(A) give Phantom jets to Israel;
(B) make the Suez canal an international waterway;
(C) send the Sixth Fleet to Haifa;
(D) attend the wedding of Moshe Dayan.

4. You are asked to speak at a St. Patrick's Day communion breakfast and the question of Social Security is raised. You suggest:
(A) breaking off all relations with Great Britain;
(B) giving Phantom jets to the IRA;
(C) sending American troops to Belfast;
(D) you reveal for the first time that you had an Irish grandmother.

Now for some *mathematical problems*. You have five minutes to solve each problem.

1. You are trying to raise money for your party to hold its national political convention. A large corporation, which has an important case pending in the Justice Department, offers you $400,000 to underwrite it. But you need $600,000. How much would another large corporation, also having trouble with the Justice Department, have to offer you to make up the difference?

2. Your campaign debts include $1,000,000 owed to the telephone company, $800,000 to the airlines, $100,000 to the printer, $50,000 to your advertising agency and $2,000 to your makeup man. How many $100-a-plate tickets would you have to sell to lobbyists to pay off your debts if you win the Presidency? How many years will it take you to pay off the debts if you lose?

Match the following:

1—Pizza	A—Jewish vote
2—Sauerbraten	B—Youth vote
3—Tamales	C—Italian vote
4—Egg foo yong	D—German vote
5—Knishes	E—Mexican vote
6—Pot	F—Chinese vote

True or false:

1—It would be impossible to win with a black Vice President.

2—Women have too many physical and psychological problems to be given positions of responsibility.

3—"Hail to the Chief" is the greatest piece of music ever written.

4—There is nothing nicer than having your daughter married in the White House.

5—If I can't be President of *all* the people, I'd rather not be President at all.

LOOKING FOR A VP

It seems that Senator George McGovern offered everyone the Vice Presidency. I became aware of this when the taxi driver who takes me to work was late.

"I'm sorry I was delayed. I just took George McGovern to his Senate office, and he asked me to run with him on the Democratic ticket."

"He did?"

"Yeah. But he was pretty honest about it. He said he had asked Senators Kennedy, Ribicoff, and Humphrey; Governor Lucey of Wisconsin; Mayor Lindsay of New York; State Senator Kalowitz of New Mexico; Alderman Hummer of Primrose, Vermont; City Councilman Rigley of Sam Hill, Idaho; Justice of the Peace Dumbottom of Long Fence, Montana; and sixteen notary publics in Detroit. They all turned him down."

"What did you say when he asked you?" I inquired.

"I told McGovern that ordinarily I would have been flattered, but I had heard through the grapevine that he had already offered the spot to his dry cleaner on MacArthur Blvd. I said I thought I should have been asked first."

"How did you know that for sure?"

"Because the check-out man at the A&P near McGovern's home told me he had been asked before the dry cleaner."

"Why didn't the A&P check-out man accept the Vice Presidency?"

"He's fooling around with a customer, the wife of someone high in government, and he's afraid it would come out."

"It probably would," I agreed. "Do you know of anyone else the Senator has talked to?"

"I know he asked the manager of the Esso gasoline station on Massachusetts Avenue. But the manager said he didn't want to give up his job because he was expecting a promotion to a much larger station on the Baltimore-Washington Expressway."

"It must be discouraging for the candidate to have so many people turn him down. He didn't ask his gardener, did he?"

"No, he wants to keep his gardener," the taxi driver said, "but he did ask his dentist."

"You mean the dentist turned it down, too?"

"The problem there, as I understand it, is the dentist has three speeding tickets on the books, and when the staff heard about it, they crossed him off the list."

"Did he ask any women that you know of?"

"His wife's hairdresser. But her husband wouldn't let her accept. McGovern seriously considered one of the women who lives on his street, but she turned out to be a Republican."

"Well, you can't say he hasn't tried," I said.

"I heard the other night he offered it to one of his Secret Servicemen."

"Which one?"

"Anyone who wanted it. But they've been around Vice Presidents a lot, and they know the job isn't much."

We arrived at the office and I paid him. Then I went upstairs. My secretary was waiting breathlessly. "George McGovern wants you to call him. It's urgent."

I placed the call.

McGovern asked, "How would you like to be my Vice President?"

"Let me say yes before you change your mind."

"Good. I'll give you Frank Mankiewicz."

Frank got on the phone. "Art, are there any skeletons in your closet?"

"You've got to be kidding!" I said. "Where do you want me to start?"

GETTING PRESS COVERAGE

When you get right down to it, the Democratic primary races were really a fight for press space and free television time. Because there were so many candidates in the race and none of them said anything new since they started running, it was very hard for a Presidential aspirant to get on the tube or in the papers unless he did something unique.

Mayor John Lindsay, for example, spent the night sleeping on the couch of a $6,000-a-year worker in Milwaukee "to identify with the little man." He was offered the worker's bed, but Lindsay said he'd rather sleep on the couch because he tossed and turned a lot at night.

As time went on, each candidate's staff had to escalate the type of stunt which attracted press and TV coverage.

I can imagine the following conversation in a candidate's office:

"Senator, we've come out with a dandy idea which will get us on the local CBS station. We've entered your wife in a roller derby Saturday night against the Bloodhawks."

"My wife can't roller skate."

"It doesn't make any difference as long as she can fight. We've set it up so Hated Hanna, the captain of the Blood-hawks, pulls your wife's hair out. Then your wife hits her in the solar plexus, and Hated Hanna will go right over the railing.

"Two other Bloodhawks will attack your wife from the rear

and start stomping on her, but her teammates will come to your wife's aid and kick the two across the rink."

"I'm not sure Penelope is up to that."

"It's essential, Senator. This state is bananas about roller derbies, and if your wife gets beaten up by the Bloodhawks, we'll pick up five percent in sympathy votes alone."

"Well, I'm going to go there to see that Penelope doesn't get hurt needlessly."

"You can't, Senator. We've booked you to perform a heart transplant at the General Hospital on the same evening."

"A heart transplant?"

"Yes, we've found a retired factory worker who says you can operate on him. It will be a good chance for you to dramatize your concern for the lack of decent medical treatment in the country. The NBC station is sending out a film crew, and Sander Vanocur will cover it live."

"All right, if you think it will help. Tell my wife I'll meet her back at the hotel after the operation."

"Oh, we forgot to tell you. You're not sleeping at the hotel Saturday night. You're sleeping at the zoo. They have a white leopard out there that everyone is crazy about, and we think if you spend a night with him, you'll get your picture on every front page in the state."

"Good grief, isn't there any *other* way of getting exposure?"

"Believe us, Senator, if there were, we wouldn't put you through all this. Now, tomorrow morning you have to be at the state fair with Penelope at nine sharp."

"That shouldn't be so difficult."

"You've been entered as a couple in the sky-diving championships."

"We're in the sky-diving championships?"

"You're not competing. You're just starting the show. Both of you jump out of a plane at two thousand feet, free fall for a thousand feet, and then yank on your parachutes. ABC bought the idea sight unseen."

"Why doesn't somebody check out these things with me before we're committed!"

"Senator, do you want to be President or don't you? After the sky-diving event, we've lined up some press exposure that no politician can buy."

"What's that?"

"We got you the lead in the touring company of *Oh! Calcutta!*"

BIG MAN, LITTLE MAN

There are two important people that all Presidential candidates must deal with if they ever hope to get any votes.

There is the big man and the little man. The big man is the candidate's source of funds, and the little man is the candidate's source of discontent. Nobody, including Richard Nixon, could win in November unless he made peace with both of them.

The president of a large corporation called in his public relations vice-president the other day and said in a fury, "What the heck is going on here? We gave this guy fifty thousand dollars and he's attacking big business."

"There's nothing to worry about, Chief. He has to attack big business to placate the little guy who is fed up with high taxes, high prices, and bureaucratic bungling. The little guy feels he has no control of his destiny."

"Well, if our man feels that strongly about the little guy, why does he come to the big guy for political campaign contributions?"

"Because, Chief, he needs the money to buy television time to attack us."

"That's just dandy. But if he feels that way, why should we give him any contribution?"

"Because, Chief, we have a lot to gain by it."

"Why do we have a lot to gain, damn it?"

"Because if the big guy doesn't give to the Presidential candidate, the candidate won't be indebted to us if he wins the election. If he isn't indebted to us, he might well carry out the promises he made to the little guy."

"It sounds pretty complicated to me. Look at this in the newspaper. Our candidate says the first thing he will do, if elected, is close all the tax loopholes and make the big guys pay what they really should."

"Exactly. If he didn't say anything about tax reform, he wouldn't have a Chinaman's chance of winning the election. We don't want to give fifty thousand dollars to a guy who is a sure loser."

"Then he says he's going to make sure the large corporations are penalized for polluting the air and water."

"The little guy digs that, Chief. He likes to believe the big guy is destroying the country."

"Well, why don't you have our candidate tell the little guy if we didn't pollute, he wouldn't have a job?"

"You don't bring that up during a Presidential election campaign. Once our man is in, then he can say it.

"Chief, I know it's not much fun to see a candidate you gave fifty thousand dollars to take you over the coals, but this is politics. The little guy still has the votes, and in order for the big guy to stay in business you have to be the heavy. Now I spoke to our candidate the other day, and he says next week he's going to attack the conglomerates and propose they be broken up."

"But we're a conglomerate!"

"That's why he told me. He says he could use twenty-five thousand dollars more to make sure the attack gets the widest distribution."

"I'm not going to give twenty-five thousand dollars to someone who wants to break up my company."

"We have to, Chief. The surveys show that the little guy fears conglomerates almost as much as busing. If our candidate's attack on conglomerates works, he could pick up one hundred delegates. I think we ought to give him the twenty-five thousand dollars to protect our fifty thousand dollars."

"And what if the little guy doesn't think breaking up conglomerates is enough?"

"Then our candidate is going to promise the little man that he'll confiscate all private property."

"Yoicks!"

$1,000 FOR EVERYONE

One of the most intriguing parts of Senator George Mc-
Govern's tax-reform plan is that he would give every man,
woman, and child in the United States $1,000 a year in cash.
The money would be taxable, and the majority of Americans
would have to return it. But those in a low enough tax bracket
or no tax bracket could keep the money as guaranteed income.

It blows one's mind to think what would happen if everyone
in this country received a check for $1,000.

It is "check" day, and Mr. and Mrs. Amberson and their
three children—Robert, seventeen, Sarah, fourteen, and Todd,
nine—have just received their $1,000 allotments from the
government with a short note:

> DEAR AMERICAN:
> Enclosed please find a $1,000 check as part of my tax
> program. If you don't need it, please send it back to the treasury,
> as we can use any surplus money you can spare.
>   Sincerely,
>   PRESIDENT GEORGE MCGOVERN

"Oh, boy," Robert says, "Now I can buy a new motorcycle."

"Wait a minute," Mr. Amberson says. "I want all those
checks. I have to pay taxes on them, and since we're in the
twenty-thousand-dollar-a-year bracket, it all must be returned
to the government."

"I'm not giving back my check," Sarah says. "It's made out
to me."

"What are you going to do with one thousand dollars,
Sarah?"

"I'm going to buy record tapes with it. There are two
hundred Rolling Stone albums I want so badly I could die."

Little Todd shouts, "Hot dog, one thousand dollars! Mom,
how much bubble gum can you get for one thousand dollars?"

"Too much," Mrs. Amberson replies. "You're not going to
spend your one thousand dollars on bubble gum."

"Sean Reilly's mom lets him spend one thousand dollars on anything he wants to. Last year he bought his own Coke machine."

"No one," Mr. Amberson shouts, "is spending any of his money on motorcycles, tapes, or bubble gum!"

"Would you believe a new washer and dryer?" Mrs. Amberson asks.

"No, not even a new washer and dryer. This is not our money. It belongs to the government," Mr. Amberson cries. "Why can't you get that through your heads?"

"Why would the government send it to us if it didn't want us to have it?" Robert demands.

"Because President McGovern believes it's easier to give one thousand dollars to everyone and then have them give it back. In this way you don't have a welfare mess."

"If I can't buy tapes with my one thousand dollars," Sarah says, "I'm going to buy an airplane ticket to Japan, and you'll never hear from me again."

Little Todd says, "I think I'll buy a color television set for my room with half of it, and with the other half I'll buy Sean Reilly's basketball cards."

"The children can do what they want with their checks," Mrs. Amberson says, "but I'm not giving this one back. I earned this one thousand dollars."

"How did you earn it?" Mr. Amberson asks.

"By working eighteen hours a day, three hundred and sixty-five days a year!"

"Please," Mr. Amberson begs, "endorse the checks and give them to me. I'll put them in the bank and on April fifteenth we'll send them back to the government. Otherwise, I'll wind up going to jail."

There is dead silence in the dining room. Suddenly Sean Reilly comes in waving his check. "Hey, Todd, I'll buy your roller skates for one thousand dollars."

"Sold," Todd says.

"Hurry up," Sean yells, "before my dad finds out where I am."

YELLING AT TV

I went over to Strybaum's house during the 1972 election
campaign about dinnertime and walked into the living room.
There was Strybaum screaming at the television set.

I looked shocked, and Ada, his wife, pulled me over to the
corner. "He's been doing that every night," Ada said. "It's
either Cronkite or Chancellor—it doesn't matter. Ever since the
election campaign started he's done nothing but yell at the set.
I'm starting to worry about him."

President Nixon came on the set, speaking at a fund-raising
dinner somewhere, and said, "And I promise that there will be
no tax raises in the next four years if I am reelected President of
the United States."

"LIAR!" Strybaum yelled. "YOU KNOW DAMN WELL
YOU'RE GOING TO HAVE TO RAISE TAXES. WHAT DO
YOU TAKE ME FOR? SOME KIND OF BLITHERING
IDIOT?"

"Strybaum," I said, "don't take it so personally. It's an
election year."

Senator McGovern came on the screen and said, "And I
promise if I am elected, I will see that the government gives
financial aid to Catholic schools."

"HORSEFEATHERS!" Strybaum shouted. (Though I must
be honest and admit he didn't say "feathers.") "YOU CAN'T
GIVE MONEY TO CATHOLIC SCHOOLS. IT'S UNCON-
STITUTIONAL, AND YOU KNOW IT, YOU BUM!"

Ada said, "Adolph, even if he can't do it, let him say he can.
He needs the votes."

Strybaum said, "I'm sick and tired of sitting here night after
night and watching these jokers lie through their teeth."

Attorney General Kleindienst came on with his big grin and
said, "I am happy to report that the crime rate is down
throughout the country, thanks to the Nixon administration's
strong law enforcement programs."

"BULLDOZER!" Strybaum yelled. "YOU CAN'T WALK

FROM YOUR OFFICE TO YOUR CAR WITHOUT GET-
TING MUGGED! WHAT KIND OF MANURE ARE YOU
HANDING OUT TO US?"

"Strybaum," I pleaded, "let the man think it if he wants to.
According to his statistics, crime is going down. He has to make
the President look good."

"We shouldn't have to put up with it," Strybaum said. "They
think they can go on the tube any time they want to and expect
us to swallow any malarkey they hand out. Well, I've had it,
and I'm going to let them know how I feel."

Sargent Shriver appeared on the screen. "And I want to tell
you, my fellow Americans, I am sick and tired of going into a
supermarket and paying thirty-seven cents for a quart of milk
so the dairy interests can fatten the Republican campaign
chest."

"WHEN WAS THE LAST TIME YOU WENT TO A
SUPERMARKET, SARGE?" Strybaum shouted. "WHEN
WAS THE LAST TIME ANY KENNEDY WAS IN A
SUPERMARKET?"

"It's hopeless," Ada said to me. "He's determined not to let
anyone get away with anything while he's watching TV."

"Strybaum," I asked, "what good does it do to yell at your
set? They can't hear you."

"They may not hear me. But if everyone in this country yells
at *his* set at the same time, they'll hear us," he replied. "Besides,
it makes me feel good. Why don't you try it?"

To placate him I said I would. John Mitchell came on the
screen and said, "I know nothing about the Watergate bugging
case, and I had nothing to do with it."

"YOU'RE LYING, JOHN!" I yelled, "AND MARTHA
KNOWS IT, TOO!"

I felt terrible.

XIII. NO MORE BOMBS

PW POWER

No one has mentioned it, but President Nixon is running out of PW's. By the end of the month, if everything goes well, all our PW's will be home. While every American will breathe a sigh of relief, the shortage of PW's will play havoc with the President's plans to bring us all together.

Ramsay Thinwhistle, an expert on the PW shortage, told me there is a great concern in Washington that without the PW issue the President will find it much more difficult to get the American people to back him in his foreign and domestic plans.

"The President has been riding high with the Americans since the PW's have been released," Thinwhistle told me. "Most people consider this his greatest triumph in ending the war and the real reason we have 'peace with honor' in Vietnam. But by April there will be no PW's to display, and Americans will start looking at the peace again and wondering what we really got out of it. It's very tough to sell the American people that we did a good thing in Vietnam when you have no more PW's coming home."

"What did you do wrong?"

"I think the big mistake," Thinwhistle replied, "is that we shouldn't have let all the PWs appear on television at the same time. We should have brought all of them back to the United States, but allowed only two or three of them to be exposed to the media every week. In that way we could have kept the PW issue alive for three years."

"That would have made more sense," I agreed.

"The truth of the matter is that the President needs the PW's now more than they need him. By rationing them to the public over a long period of time, Mr. Nixon could keep the amnesty issue alive, he could appeal to the patriotism of the American people, and he could use the PWs to attack all the people who don't agree with him. They are a natural administration resource, and it's a pity we used them up so fast."

"You should have thought of that when they first started arriving at Clark Field," I said.

"I agree," Thinwhistle said, "but we were caught up in the emotional excitement of the moment. In other wars we have had thousands of PW's but we never made any use of them for political purposes. In fact, this is the first war in American history where PW's have been used to prove we won.

"Frankly we didn't realize the impact the PW release would have. We brought five hundred thousand men back from Vietnam, and the American people didn't give a tinker's damn about any of them. But the five hundred sixty-two PW's were something else again. The people identified with them and their families. They were the only heroes to come out of this war. If we had known what they really meant to the American people, I assure you we wouldn't have given them to TV all at the same time."

"It's too late to do anything about it?" I said.

"It's too late to do anything about these PW's, but if you recall at last week's press conference the President hinted that if Hanoi kept violating the truce agreement, he might be forced to start bombing again."

"But if he starts bombing again, won't that mean that the President will be making more PW's?" I asked.

"Exactly. The more bombing you do in the north, the more

PW's you give to Hanoi. If North Vietnam doesn't see the light, we could have five hundred sixty-two PW's in their camps by Christmas."

"Then that would take care of the PW shortage?"

"We don't want it, and we're not provoking it. But bombing does mean PW's, and we're going to bring them home if it takes us four more years."

UNAUTHORIZED TO LEAK

No one seemed to be more distraught over the release of the Pentagon Papers than the famed hawk columnist Joseph Wallstop.

When I visited Joe in his bunker underneath his house in Georgetown, Joe was frothing at the mouth.

"They were my papers," Joe cried. "The New York *Times* and Washington *Post* had no right to use them."

I look confused. "How could they be your papers, Joe? I thought they belonged to the Pentagon."

"I have had a deal with three administrations to get first crack at all top-secret classified documents."

"Why you, Joe?"

"Because I am a friend of the Pentagon, because I believe in the war, because when they leak a document to me, they know it will be printed the way they wrote it. Now everyone has access to top secret material. It's not fair."

"Are you trying to tell me, Joe, that the Pentagon Papers aren't the first classified documents that got into the papers?"

"You must be a fool," Joe replied contemptuously. "Every one of my columns is based on top secret information. The administration's quarrel with the leaking of the Pentagon Papers is not with what was revealed in them, but who printed them."

"Joe, if I hear you right, the government has been leaking classified documents to friendly newspapermen for years."

"I don't know how I can make it any clearer," Joe said in his usual irritated voice.

"Then what did the New York *Times* and Washington *Post* do that was so wrong?"

"They printed *unauthorized* leaks of classified documents. The leaks that I have printed have been authorized by the highest men in government. When they give me a top secret paper, I know they want to see it in the papers. For one thing it shows them in a good light, which is very important if you're a high government official. The Pentagon Papers show high officials in a bad light, and that, my friend, no matter how you look at it, is treason."

"Maybe Daniel Ellsberg didn't know the New York *Times* and Washington *Post* were unauthorized to receive government secrets."

"He knew it all right," Joe said. "And if there was any question, he should have checked with the Joint Chiefs of Staff. They have a top secret list of newspapermen who can have access to classified documents. I can assure you that no one from the New York *Times* or the Washington *Post* is on that list."

"I can understand why you're mad, Joe. But is there anything you can do about it?"

"I certainly can. Since the Pentagon Papers were printed, I have received hundreds of top secret classified documents from sources I cannot reveal, proving the Pentagon Papers are wrong."

"But how does the reader know your top-secret papers are more accurate than Ellsberg's top secret papers?"

"Because mine were leaked to me by responsible men who have no ax to grind except to prove the decisions they made were right," Joe said.

"That makes sense. Wouldn't the government be wise to list the newspapermen they were leaking papers to so the public knows who to trust?"

"I don't think you have to go that far," Joe said. "The best test for the public when reading a secret document is: If it supports the government, it's an authorized leak, and if it doesn't, it's a matter for the Justice Department and a grand jury."

The doorbell rang, and a four-star general handed Joe a large brown envelope. "These are your columns for next week, Mr. Wallstop. Please sign here."

NO AMNESTY

One of the hottest emotional words being bandied about these days is "amnesty." Both President Nixon and Vice President Agnew have vowed never to give amnesty to those who refused to go and fight for freedom in Vietnam. But amnesty means all things to all people.

Cedric Farfinkle, an acquaintance by marriage, told me, "I am against amnesty for anyone who got us involved in Vietnam."

"That's rather harsh, Cedric."

"Nevertheless, there is no reason to forgive anyone who cost this country forty-five thousand lives and one hundred fifty billion dollars."

"Christian charity says you should forgive people after a war is over," I protested.

"These men knew what they were doing. They had a choice, and without consulting Congress or anyone, they got us in the war. There should be a public stigma applied to them. They shouldn't be allowed to go off to teach at Harvard, head up banks and law firms, and write books without some kind of punishment," Farfinkle said.

"That's easy for you to say. These men had the choice of going into Vietnam or staying out of it," I said. "The fact that they chose to go in is to their credit. They may have violated the law, but sometimes you have to put your conscience above the law."

"You're talking like a bleeding heart," Farfinkle said. "Suppose we forgave everybody who got us into a war. How would that look to the young people of this country?"

"I may be a bleeding heart, Farfinkle," I said, "but I still believe that no matter what a man did during a war, he should not have to carry it around with him the rest of his life."

"I'm not asking for a blanket punishment for all the people

who got us into this war," Farfinkle said. "I think each case should be taken on its own merits. There are probably some people who can prove extenuating circumstances, and we might forgive them after a hearing. But what I say is that granting general amnesty for all the men responsible for getting us into this war would be a travesty of justice and would demean the great number of people who have fought for ten years to get us out."

"Everyone makes mistakes," I cried. "Just because a man did what he felt was the right thing at the time does not make him guilty of a war crime."

"Maybe so," Farfinkle said, "but I don't think these war-makers should be allowed to just come back and take up their lives where they left off. Perhaps at some future date, after all the emotions have calmed down, some President might pardon them. But for now they should be made to pay the price for their actions. If we grant amnesty, they won't even realize they did anything wrong."

I was getting discouraged. "Every country in the world forgives the people who start a war once the peace agreement is signed. Without that, no one would have faith in his leaders."

"No amnesty," Farfinkle said.

"What kind of punishment would you propose for those who got us into and kept us in the war?"

"I would forbid them to vote or hold public office. I would also make them serve for two years in some government peace organization to prove they've had a change of mind."

"But, Farfinkle," I said, "what you're proposing to do would punish the cream of the American Establishment. If given amnesty, some of these men may turn out to be fine, upstanding citizens."

"They're going to have to go some," Farfinkle said, "to prove it to me."

"OH, WHAT A LOUSY WAR"

When President Nixon announced the cease-fire in Vietnam,

there was little rejoicing in the land. The trouble is that Vietnam has given *all* wars a bad name.

Howard Sufferman and a small group of concerned citizens in this country have started a War Anti-Defamation League which hopes to dispel the prejudices against war caused by our adventure in Indochina.

Sufferman told me, "I don't think people should judge all wars by Vietnam. Of course, there are always a few rotten ones in any barrel, but the majority of wars are upstanding, patriotic events that most Americans can be proud of."

"What do you think went wrong with this war?" I asked Sufferman.

"For one thing," he replied, "the good guys and the bad guys looked alike. You really can't have a good war when both your enemies and your allies have slanted eyes."

"But the bad guys did wear black pajamas," I pointed out.

"No matter," Sufferman said, "it was hard for Americans watching TV every night to get steamed up about a bunch of little runts who were five feet tall and weighed sixty-five pounds. What the hell kind of enemy is that?"

"Terrible casting," I agreed.

"I knew the war could never work," Sufferman said, "when no one on Tin Pan Alley wrote a war song to get the blood boiling and the juices flowing."

"It's hard to make anything rhyme with 'protective reaction strike,' " I said.

"And Hollywood let us down miserably," Sufferman added. "In order to have a good war, you have to have dozens of motion pictures showing our brave American boys with their backs to the wall wiping out hundreds and hundreds of the ruthless yellow enemy. If you want to know the truth, what we missed more than anything was Errol Flynn. Perhaps if he were alive and we had put him on the Ho Chi Minh Trail with a machine gun and five hand grenades, the entire attitude toward Vietnam might have been different."

"We had John Wayne," I reminded Sufferman.

"Americans are more sophisticated now," he replied. "One film on the Green Berets is not enough to sell the people on a war."

"What else went wrong in your opinion?"

"We didn't have rationing," Sufferman said. "The American people like to make sacrifices during a war—they want to be part of it. We had no scrap drives, no blackout curtains, no posters warning the enemy was listening. War is no fun if you don't feel a part of it. Even if the U.S. government didn't need it, they should have asked people to contribute string and tinfoil."

Sufferman continued, "There were so many mistakes I can't even list them all. A good war requires armies to fight for real estate. When the Pentagon decided to make enemy body counts the standard of whether we were winning or not, the American people lost interest. We wanted names of hills and valleys, towns and hamlets that our boys had valiantly fought for. And all they gave us was numbers of enemy killed. The whole thing became a bloody bore."

"Maybe the next war will be better," I said.

"I hope so," Sufferman said. "A couple more lousy ones like Vietnam, and you're going to get the American people turned off on war for good."

HE HEARD THE WHOLE THING

"I can't believe I heard the *whole* thing!"

"You heard it, Ralph."

"I can't believe I heard the *whole* thing!"

"Ralph, take an Alka-Seltzer and go to bed."

"Did he really say he was going to mine the Haiphong Harbor and bomb all the railroads around Hanoi?"

"He said it, Ralph. Now go to sleep."

"Did he really say it's up to the Soviet Union to get us out of the war?"

"I heard him, Ralph. That's what he said. He said we were more than generous with our peace offer, and all the other side did was commit naked aggression."

"Naked aggression? Oh, my stomach is killing me."

"I told you to take an Alka-Seltzer and go to bed."

"I've taken four Alka-Seltzers, it doesn't help. I can't believe I heard the *whole* thing."

"Ralph, maybe it's not that bad. Maybe the mines that were dropped around Haiphong were made by the same people who put out the GM and Ford cars that had to be recalled. Maybe the mines will have to be recalled, too."

"You're just trying to cheer me up. I knew he'd do something stupid if he saw *Patton* more than four times."

"Ralph! That's no way to talk about the President of the United States! He has asked for our support in this great hour of crisis."

"I've been supporting him. Don't you remember that I hung out the American flag during his invasion of Cambodia? That didn't do a damn bit of good."

"But, Ralph, he had to do it, or no President of the United States would be able to travel around the globe with respect anymore."

"Suppose there is no globe to travel around?"

"Ralph, the President knows what he's doing. He's being advised by the Pentagon, and they haven't been wrong on the war so far. Turn out the lights."

"Maybe we should order blackout curtains?"

"Ralph, you're overreacting. The President has the situation under control. Henry Kissinger wouldn't let him do it if it weren't safe."

"I think I'll write a letter to my Senator."

"It doesn't do any good, Ralph. Nixon doesn't ask the Senate what he should do when the honor of the United States is at stake."

"Who does he ask?"

"Billy Graham and Bob Hope."

"I can't believe I heard the *whole* thing."

"Ralph, you heard it. I saw you hearing it. Take another Alka-Seltzer and try to dream that Johnson is still President."

"Suppose it doesn't work? Suppose the North Vietnamese succeed in their offensive? What will he do then?"

"He's got a secret plan, Ralph. That's why he's President. If this doesn't work, the Joint Chiefs of Staff will present him with a whole new set of options, and you know what they'll say to the President?"

"What?"

"They'll say, 'Try it. You'll like it.'"

PICTURES FROM VIETNAM

The President was sitting in his Oval Office when Henry Kissinger walked in.

"Say, Henry, these photographs of the moon are fantastic."

"They're not photographs of the moon, Mr. President, they're the latest aerial pictures from South Vietnam."

"Vietnam?"

"Yes, sir. There are now fifty-two million craters in South Vietnam. By the end of the year we should go over the one hundred million mark."

"That's great, Henry. But I don't see any towns in the photographs."

"Here. You see this series of rock outcroppings? That was a town. And over here, this bleak, flat, open space—that was a town. And here where this giant hole is—that's a provincial capital."

"Well, you could have fooled me. There doesn't seem to be much green in the photographs."

"No, sir, Mr. President. The defoliation program took care of the green. But you notice there's lots of gray."

"What does that signify, Henry?"

"Our B-52 pacification program is working. Green means cover for the North Vietnamese. Gray means they have to fight in the open. The more gray on the photographs, the better chance we have of turning back naked aggression."

"What are these brown streaks here?"

"They used to be roads, Mr. President. But you can't call them that anymore."

"I guess you can't. Where are the hamlets where we have won the hearts and minds of the people?"

"Most of them are in these blue areas, underwater. We had to bomb the dams so the enemy couldn't capture the rice."

"Uh-huh. I see there are a lot of black areas in the photos. Does that signify anything?"

"Yes, sir. It means our scorched earth policy is working. Every black area on this photograph means the North Vietnamese have been deprived of supplies and shelter. We've left them nothing."

"Good thinking, Henry. Where are the people?"

"What people, Mr. President?"

"The people we're defending against an imposed Communist government."

"You can't see them in the photographs. They're hiding in the craters."

"And the South Vietnamese army?"

"They're hiding in these craters over here."

"I see. I wish these photographs could be printed in Hanoi. It would certainly give the North Vietnamese something to think about."

"So do I, Mr. President. Now, this area over here by the sea still has some green in it."

"I was going to ask you about that, Henry."

"The Navy assures me that it should be gray and black in three weeks. It's the type of terrain that lends itself better to shelling than to bombing."

"Well, Henry, I want you to know I believe these are excellent photographs, and I want you to send a 'well done' cable to everyone responsible. The only thing that worries me is what happens if we get a cease-fire? Isn't it going to be awfully expensive to make everything green again?"

"Don't worry, Mr. President, we've thought of that. We've asked for bids from the companies who make artificial turf. Once the shooting stops, we're going to carpet South Vietnam from wall to wall."

SO I MADE A MISTAKE

It is perhaps fifteen years since I have seen my Spanish friend Enrique Hombria. He embraces me like this, kisses me on both cheeks like this, and then he says with pride in his voice, "My friend, you will not recognize Madrid since you were here before."

Enrique takes me out to the car in the large airport parking lot. "We have parking lots now just like you have in the United States," he says proudly.

"That's nice," I tell him.

We start driving into the city. "You see," he says, "we have superhighways just like in America."

The traffic gets thicker, and the cars are bumper to bumper. The buses are spewing out smoke, and as we drive slowly into the city, a smog can be seen over the city.

"It's different, huh, my friend?" Enrique says, almost hitting two young people on a motorcycle.

"Very different, Enrique."

"Wait until you see the buildings. We are building everywhere." Enrique is not lying. There is office building after office building, apartment house after apartment house, some beautiful, most ugly cement boxes making a harsh new skyline.

"How do you like?" Enrique asks.

"I'm floored," I say honestly.

"I remember fifteen years ago," Enrique says, "you said to me, 'Enrique, in order to be a great country and a happy one, you must become an industrial power.'"

"I said that?"

"*Sí,* and you said Spain must have automobiles, and new roads and large buildings and factories, because that is how you become a proud and contented people. Look, over there is a Revlon factory, there is a Coca-Cola plant, there is a Dodge factory, there is 3M's, now we pass Squibb and RCA. What do you think of my Spain now?"

"My friend," I say gently, "I don't know how to break this to you. But I was wrong."

"Wrong about what?"

"I was wrong fifteen years ago when I told you in order to be happy, you had to be a great industrial power. We have finally discovered in America that the simple life is the best life."

"You mean we shouldn't have built the roads, the buildings,

the factories, the automobiles, the hotels, the credit card systems?" Enrique asks, puzzled.

"I'm afraid not," I reply. "You will discover, as we have, that automobiles and office buildings and superhighways and credit cards will bring you nothing but trouble."

"But," Enrique says, his arm sweeping out across the Madrid skyline, "you told us to build all this. You said all this would bring us happiness."

"Anyone can make a mistake," I reply defensively.

Enrique is crestfallen as we creep along in the traffic breathing the fumes of the other cars. "What do we do now?"

"Go back to the simple life, Enrique, get yourself a jug of wine and a loaf of bread and a burro. That is the only true happiness."

Enrique slams the steering wheel of his car. "NOW HE TELLS ME!"

BOMBING THE DIKES

Was the United States bombing the dikes in North Vietnam or wasn't it? That was the question. President Nixon and Secretary of Defense Laird said we were not. The Secretary-general of the United Nations, the president of the World Council of Churches, and Jane Fonda said we were.

Whom was one to believe?

To find an answer to the problem, I called Wellback Fishbind, the world's leading authority on dike bombing.

Wellback told me, "I believe both sides are telling the truth. The Americans are not bombing the dikes in North Vietnam, but the dikes are being bombed by the Americans."

"How can that be?"

"The Americans have strict orders to bomb only military installations, power plants, and moving targets. They have specific orders not to bomb the dikes. Therefore, President Nixon and Secretary of Defense Laird are telling the truth.

"Unfortunately, these dikes are located next to the military targets. So, when the Americans bomb the military sites, they can't help hitting the dikes. The Secretary-general of the United Nations, the president of the World Council of Churches, and Jane Fonda, therefore, are also telling the truth."

"But there seems to be a credibility gap somewhere," I protested.

"It depends on where you are. If you're sitting in the White House, you obviously feel the North Vietnamese should build their dikes farther away from their military targets, so American planes won't hit them.

"But if you're in a bomb shelter in North Vietnam, you feel that the dikes built close to military sites should be spared."

Wellback said, "The thing to keep in mind is that no one likes to bomb dikes. There's very little satisfaction in it. You hit an oil refinery with a bomb, and you get a helluva thrill out of seeing it go up with a whoosh. But when you hit a dike, the bomb lands with a dull thud, and you have no idea if you're doing any good or not. It's the same thing with a dam. There's no thrill to shooting rockets at a dam. But if you can shoot up a military barracks or a moving convoy, you know you're earning your money."

"I never thought of it like that."

"As I see it," Wellback said, "it's really North Vietnam's problem. They have too many dikes. It's almost impossible to hit anything worthwhile in the country without hitting a dike. The way the North Vietnamese can avoid having their dikes bombed is to take them down so we can't destroy them."

"That would be one solution," I agreed.

"It isn't our fault that Hanoi built so many dikes. We'd be grateful if they didn't have any at all. They're absolutely useless to us. As a matter of fact, they're hurting our entire bombing strategy."

"But if they didn't have dikes their land would flood."

"That's their problem. Do you know that not one country club in North Vietnam has been destroyed by our bombing? Why do you think that is?"

"I have no idea."

"Because there isn't a country club in North Vietnam. Now, if they didn't have any dikes in North Vietnam, then we wouldn't destroy any, would we?"

"I guess not," I said.

"Since the North Vietnamese insist on having dikes, and we insist on bombing North Vietnam," Wellback said, "we won't stop bombing until they pull out their dikes, and they won't stop building dikes until we stop the bombing."

"That sounds like an impasse," I said.

"Exactly. And there is nothing to prevent us from bombing impasses. President Nixon has made that perfectly clear."

THE HIGH COST OF BOMBING

If all goes well with the peace accords, it will just be a matter of time before the United States sends a team of damage experts to Hanoi to estimate what it will cost to rebuild North Vietnam. The price tag last year was $2.5 billion, but this was before the carpet bombing of Hanoi and Haiphong at Christmas.

I can see the U.S. team of experts arriving at the Hanoi airport and being greeted by Ho Gap, the North Vietnamese Minister for Reconstruction.

The minister says, "Welcome to our humble country. Forgive us for the condition of our airport, which unfortunately was destroyed by your excellent and talented Air Force."

"We did all this?" one of the damage experts asks.

"Yes, but please do not apologize. We know the airport you will build us will more than make up for it. What we think we'd like is something on the order of Dulles near Washington, D.C. Our engineers estimate that with Communist labor it should not cost more than forty million dollars, give or take ten million dollars, for what I believe you people refer to as 'overruns.'"

"Can't we talk about this later?" one of the U.S. damage experts asks. "We'd like to go to our hotel and get cleaned up."

"Of course," the minister replies, "forgive me for thoughtlessness. Please get in the trucks, and we will take you there."

"Trucks?"

"Alas," the minister says, "our private automobiles were all destroyed in your protective reaction strikes of December fifteenth. But we have plans to build a new automobile factory to produce the four-door Ho Chi Minh with a Wankel engine. We think we can undersell the Japanese in America by five hundred dollars a car. Here, you can study the plans in your spare time."

The U.S. damage control team climbs on board the trucks.

"How far is it into town?" one of the Americans asks.

"Ordinarily, twenty minutes. But, unfortunately, the Bridge of Peace and Conciliation Heartbreak was hit by a 'smart bomb' from one of your B-52's, and therefore, it will take two hours," the minister says.

"I suppose you want us to pay for the bridge, too," a damage control expert says.

"We thought you might build us a tunnel instead. Something like the Lincoln or Holland tunnels, which we understand work quite well."

"Was that the only bridge destroyed?"

"Oh, dear, I wish it was! According to your own Air Force estimates, you destroyed three thousand four hundred fifty-seven bridges, all of which were listed as military targets."

"But you people don't have that many bridges in all North Vietnam!"

"That's what we kept telling the U.S. Air Force. But they kept destroying them anyway."

The truck passed a building with only the walls standing.

"What was that?" one of the damage experts asks.

"That was the Anti-Imperialist Shirt and Textile Factory. Your intelligence people kept referring to it as an ammunition dump."

"What's that going to cost us?" one of the Americans asks.

"Well," says the minister, "we thought as long as we have to rebuild the factory, we'd go in for automation and work in synthetic fibers. We believe that with American help we could be producing Arrow-type shirts for the United States in less than three years. I think we put you down for eighty million dollars for a new plant."

"Damn," says one of the damage experts, "we haven't even gotten to the hotel yet, and with the bridges they're up to two billion dollars."

Finally the truck pulls up in front of the ruins of a

dilapidated building with boarded-up windows and sides held up by scaffolding.

"Here we are, gentlemen," the minister says.

"*This* is the hotel?" one of the damage men asks incredulously.

"This is it," the minister says. "It was hit by a rocket on Christmas Day. As soon as you wash up in the river over there, we'd like to discuss with you our fantastic plans for a new super Kissinger Hilton."

THE REASON WHY

The Why Are We in Vietnam Committee, otherwise known as WAWIVNC, held its monthly meeting at the State Department, and for the first time there was an air of pessimism in the room. As everyone knows, WAWIVNC was set up many years ago to provide Presidents of the United States with solid reasons for American involvement in Vietnam.

Some of the reasons the committee has come up with in the past are:

A. To halt Communist aggression from the North.

B. To let Red China know we mean business.

C. To prevent Southeast Asian countries from falling like dominoes.

D. To keep American boys from having to fight on the shores of Hawaii.

E. To prove to Hanoi we are not a helpless giant.

F. To make sure the South Vietnamese people can choose their own leaders in democratic elections.

This last one was everyone's favorite. President Nixon kept repeating it in every speech about Indochina. Secretary of State Rogers, Ambassador Ellsworth Bunker in Saigon, and Ambassador David Bruce in Paris all said the same thing: "The United States wants nothing for itself. It is only in South Vietnam to assure that the people there can decide their own fate."

You can imagine what happened at the WAWIVNC meeting

when they were informed that President Thieu would be the only one on the ballot in the Presidential elections on October 3.

The chairman of the committee said, "Gentlemen, I have just heard from President Nixon. He is very disappointed that no one has chosen to run against President Thieu and is once again hard put to explain what the United States is doing in Vietnam."

"Well, it isn't our fault that Vice President Ky wouldn't run against Thieu, or that General Minh bowed out of the race weeks ago," an assistant secretary of public affairs said.

"How did we know that Thieu would rig the elections so badly that even the opposition would see through him?" a USIA psychological warfare expert said.

"Thieu should have warned Ky and Minh that they either had to run against him in democratic elections or they would be shot," a CIA man said.

"That's not the point, gentlemen," the chairman of the committee said. "The fact is that Thieu is running alone. This is not our concern except that since it's now difficult for President Nixon to defend the American presence in Vietnam to guarantee free elections, we have to find him another reason to explain why we are still there. Now think."

"Suppose," an AID man said, "the President says the reason we are in Vietnam is to protect the American dollar?"

"I don't follow you."

"Well, we all know every high official in the South Vietnamese government has a secret Swiss bank account where he has stashed away millions of dollars. Now, if these officials traded their dollars in Switzerland for marks or French francs while the dollar is floating, it could hurt us badly.

"But as long as we remain in South Vietnam, these officials will have faith in us and will keep their dollars in Switzerland."

"It's too complicated," the chairman said. "I want something simple."

"Suppose we say we're in Vietnam because we must protect freedom wherever it is found," a Pentagon man said.

There was dead silence in the room.

Finally the chairman said, "There has to be a reason that no one has yet thought of."

A State Department man scribbled something on a sheet of paper and then raised his hand. "This is it. The President must go on television tomorrow night and tell the American people the only reason we are in Vietnam is because it's there."

MR. NIXON AGAINST THE WALL

Dr. Kis N Guh, President Thieu's special representative, has arrived here with his top advisers to try to persuade President Nixon to form a coalition government in the United States.

So far the talks have not been going well, and President Nixon has remained adamant in his stand not to accept a negotiated settlement of the November elections.

"I intend to remain President for the next four years," President Nixon angrily told Dr. Kis N Guh, "no matter how much pressure the South Vietnamese government puts on me."

Dr. Kis N Guh told President Nixon, "This is completely unsatisfactory to the Democratic Party. They insist that peace can only come to the United States if you are removed from office. We, of course, will support you, but we have to reach some compromise that will be satisfactory to all parties."

"No compromise," President Nixon said. "I will not make one concession to the Democrats. They are trying to destroy my government, and I will not stand for it."

"Before you make up your mind, let me spell out the terms of a peaceful settlement to see if something can be worked out," Dr. Kis N Guh said. "President Thieu considers them very reasonable and urges you to accept them."

President Nixon sat stony-faced.

"First," said Dr. Kis N Guh, "you would remain President of the United States until the country holds free and open elections under international supervision."

"That's ridiculous," said President Nixon.

Dr. Kis N Guh continued, "Second, Senator George Mc-

Govern would be named Vice President in the coalition government."

"What about Spiro Agnew?" President Nixon demanded.

"He would become the U.S. ambassador to Uganda," Dr. Kis N Guh replied, "Ramsey Clark would be Attorney General, and Dr. Spock would be Secretary of Health, Education, and Welfare."

"What about my people?" President Nixon asked.

"Your people would have Cabinet positions, too. James Hoffa would be Secretary of Transportation, and Maurice Stans would be Secretary of the Treasury. The rest of the Cabinet posts would go to Ralph Nader's people, whom we consider at this moment neutral."

"What else have you thought up for me?" President Nixon asked testily.

"After the cease-fire, all territory pacified by the Republicans will remain Republican and all territory in Democratic hands will stay Democratic.

"Now this is the part we think you'll like. The Democrats have agreed to give amnesty to all Republicans involved in the Watergate bugging scandal on the condition that every tape and captured enemy document be returned to Democratic headquarters."

"We're winning the war," President Nixon said. "I see no reason why we should bargain with outlaws."

"I cannot stress," Dr. Kis N Guh said, "how strongly President Thieu feels this is a just and honorable settlement. *His* election depends on achieving peace in the United States. He has asked me to tell you that if you do not accept the conditions as outlined, he will not accept any more military and civilian aid for his country."

"Why, that's blackmail," President Nixon said.

"President Thieu has also told me to advise you that unless you agree to a coalition government, he will not allow you to bomb North Vietnam."

"He's taking all my options away!" President Nixon cried.

"It's up to you," Dr. Kis N Guh said. "President Thieu is losing his patience, and the people of South Vietnam are sick and tired of all the fighting going on in the United States. What is your answer?"

"Tell President Thieu," President Nixon said, "that no matter how much I need to support him, if he tries to force this settlement on me, I will go it alone."

WHEN PEACE IS AT HAND

When he came back to the United States after his peace talks in Paris, the first thing Henry Kissinger did was report to President Nixon at the Waldorf Towers.

"How was Paris, Henry?"

"Great, Mr. President. They have a new show at the Folies Bergères and—"

"I'm talking about the peace negotiations, Henry."

"Oh, yes. I think peace is at hand. It's just a question of buttoning down a few points."

"Good. Did Le Duc Tho agree to change the draft of the cease-fire agreement?"

"No, he didn't. He said he was sticking by the original nine-point plan, and his people wouldn't budge an inch."

"I see. What did Thieu's people say about that?"

"They said that unless the entire agreement was rewritten, Saigon would not budge an inch."

"It sounds like a stalemate to me, Henry."

"That's how it sounds to me, too."

"What do we do now, Henry?"

"I thought you might have some ideas, Mr. President."

"I thought *you* had some ideas, Henry."

"Well, why don't I go back to Paris and tell Hanoi that unless they change the agreement, we will be forced to back President Thieu?"

"That's a thought."

"And then why don't I tell Thieu unless he agrees to the accord as it is presently written, we will be forced to back Hanoi?"

"Let me get this straight, Henry. We're telling the North Vietnamese that they have to change the agreement and the South Vietnamese they have to accept it without changes?"

"Exactly."

"That sort of confuses me, Henry."

"Well, if it confuses you, just think what it will do to them."

"Do you have any other ideas, Henry?"

"We got the North Vietnamese to agree to a peace settlement by bombing Hanoi and mining Haiphong Harbor. Since the South Vietnamese seem to be the stumbling block right now, why not bomb Saigon and mine Cam Ranh Bay?"

"But we can't bomb Saigon. Think of world opinion."

"We can't officially, Mr. President. But suppose we reactivated Air Force General Lavelle and gave him very vague orders as to what he could or could not bomb in South Vietnam?"

"But if we mine the harbors of South Vietnam, how do we get Thieu the military aid we promised him?"

"Through North Vietnam, Mr. President. We sweep the mines out of Haiphong Harbor and ship our supplies in that way."

"Why would the North Vietnamese allow us to ship our supplies to South Vietnam through Haiphong?"

"That's the only part I haven't figured out yet, Mr. President, but I have my people working on it."

"Do you have any other idea, Henry?"

"I have one more plan. You announce that a peace agreement has been reached with both the North and South Vietnamese, and then we pull out."

"You mean announce it, even if it isn't true?"

"It's your word against theirs, Mr. President."

"That's all you've got, Henry?"

"That's it, Mr. President. There's only one more idea. What about implementing your secret plan to end the war in 1968?"

"All right, go ahead with it."

"Fine. What is the plan? You know you never told me."

"I'm sorry, Henry, I can't tell you. There are some things a President must keep to himself."

WARCE IS AT HAND

It seemed obvious from the Kissinger talks in Paris that we were unable to work out a true peace treaty in Vietnam.

Hallaby Hegelstein, a political science professor, maintains the most we can get out of Indochina is a "warce."

"What is a warce?" I asked him.

"It is neither peace nor war; it is actually a combination of both. For some time now the world has needed a new word to describe the situation many countries are in. In the Middle East you do not have peace, nor do you have a fighting war. The English language has no word for this predicament, so I invented one which I call 'warce.' "

"How would warce apply to Vietnam?"

"If the United States signs a treaty with Hanoi which the South Vietnamese refuse to ratify, you will have a state of warce. President Nixon may call it a peace, but he would only be kidding himself and the American people."

"What would the warce consist of?" I asked.

"You would probably have a cease-fire with some fighting on both sides. The North Vietnamese and Vietcong will continue sporadic probing of the South Vietnamese defenses, and the South Vietnamese will probably make occasional attacks on Vietcong strongholds. But both sides will probably be stalemated, and the warce could continue for years."

"Well, I guess a warce in Indochina is better than nothing," I said.

"It might be the coming thing. Since peace treaties are so hard to come by, I would advocate that nations sign warce treaties instead. It could save face on both sides. Many of our world leaders consider the signing of a peace pact a sign of weakness. But no one could criticize them at home if they said they had agreed to a warce."

"I imagine if he couldn't have it any other way, President Nixon would settle for a generation of warce," I said.

"The advantage of warce," Hegelstein said, "is that Congress wouldn't have to declare it. If the President decided he wanted to involve the country in a warce, he could do it on his own."

"And if he succeeded," I said, "he could be nominated for the Nobel Warce Prize."

"I believe the nation would thrive on a warce footing," Hegelstein said. "You wouldn't have to shut down your defense plants and put a lot of people out of work, and at the same time you would use very little of the stuff to kill people."

"And you could sell warce bonds to finance it," I added.

"It would also solve the military problem. In a period of peace, the armed forces find themselves in disrepute. But if we were at warce, our men in uniform would still be respected and there would be plenty of opportunity for promotion," Hegelstein said.

He added, "The world is not ready for peace and may never be. At the same time, war is not the answer to our problems. Therefore, we must condition ourselves to warce—whether they be warces of liberation, limited warces, or even a world warce. Vietnam may be the big test. If we can have a successful warce there, it will prove that it's possible to have a warce anywhere."

"That's a good thought to leave with people at this time of year, Professor."

"Thank you. Merry Christmas, and remember, warce on earth—goodwill to men."

THE NOBEL PEACE PRIZE

"The Nobel Peace Prize Committee will come to order. We will now start examining the list of candidates. Who is first, Mr. Secretary?"

"Richard M. Nixon. His name has been submitted by U.S. Senator Hugh Scott."

"We can't have Nixon, not after the bombing attacks he ordered on North Vietnam last Christmas."

"*Au contraire,* Mr. President. I think Richard Nixon is a very suitable candidate for the Peace Prize. He is eliminating the B-52 from the United States' arsenal of weapons."

"How is he doing that?"

"He is having them shot down by the enemy. The United States had only one hundred B-52's. So far twelve have been shot down. At the rate they are going, they will all disappear in three months. What better gesture can one make toward peace?"

"It's out of the question, gentlemen. Nixon has bombed hospitals and schools and killed thousands of innocent civilians. We cannot give him the Peace Prize for this."

"But wait a minute. Does he not get credit for restraint? After all, he hasn't used atomic weapons against the North Vietnamese. A man who has the hydrogen bomb and doesn't use it against an enemy should certainly get the prize or at least an honorable mention."

"I do not dispute that, but the Nobel Peace Prize has certain stipulations to it, and one is you do not award it to a man who has dropped more bombs on North Vietnam than have been dropped in all of World War Two."

"Yes, Mr. President, but we must remember the *only* reason Nixon is bombing the North Vietnamese is to achieve a generation of peace for all mankind. If this bombing were punitive, then I would say scratch him off the list. But Nixon is trying to find peace through bombing, and he should be honored for it."

"I object. Nixon has been trying to achieve peace through bombing for four years. It hasn't worked, and it will not work. If we award the prize to a man who believes the only solution to peace is destroying the other side, we will be the laughingstock of the world."

"What does the world know? Nixon has said he will stop the bombing any time the North Vietnamese come to the negotiating table and agree to a fair and just settlement of the war. I say a man who talks that way has gone the extra mile."

"But what is a fair and just settlement of the war?"

"That is not for this committee to decide, Mr. President. For years now, we have given the Peace Prize to people who have done a great deal of talking about peace, but have had no effect on anybody. This time we have a candidate who has done *something* about peace."

"What has he done?"

"He has shown everyone that he is dead serious about peace, even if he has to commit his entire Air Force and Navy to bring it about."

"That's true, Olav. But at the same time, wouldn't it be better to wait until the bombing stops before we give Nixon the Peace Prize?"

"By then it could be too late, particularly if he hasn't achieved peace in time. Don't you see what a fine gesture it would be if we gave the prize to a man who was working for peace but hadn't quite made it?"

"We could be at this all day, gentlemen. Let's go on to the next candidate for the peace prize. Mr. Secretary, what is the second name on the list?"

"Henry Kissinger."

"Oh, boy."

WHERE WERE YOU, DADDY?

It must have been very tough for a Congressman or Senator, when he came home at night, to explain to his teen-age children what was going on in Vietnam.

"Daddy, where were you when they were bombing the cities of Hanoi and Haiphong?"

"I was in recess, and you damn well know it."

"But why don't you protest now?"

"Because it would hurt the sensitive negotiations going on in Paris, which hopefully will lead to a just peace in Indochina."

"Why didn't you protest before?"

"Because I didn't want to hurt the sensitive negotiations that have been going on for the last four years which would lead to an honorable peace in Indochina."

"But didn't you see all the photographs of civilians being killed and hospitals being destroyed?"

"Damn it, son! You don't understand the role of Congress. We're supposed to support the President during war. If we oppose the war, we will be giving aid and comfort to the enemy."

"But I thought Congress was supposed to declare war."

"Who told you that?"

"It's in the Constitution."

"Now don't believe *everything* you learn in school. Technically it's true that Congress should declare war, but you see we're not really at war. It's a police action."

"When does a police action become a war?"

"When the President asks for an official declaration. Since three Presidents have not asked us to declare war, there is no reason for us to do so."

"Doesn't Congress have any say in what the President can do in Indochina?"

"Of course it does. The President has to ask for our advice and consent before he makes any major decisions which involve the lives of American boys and the expenditure of billions of dollars."

"Well, why hasn't he done it?"

"He probably forgot."

"All the kids at school say Congress is afraid to act on the war."

"A lot they know. Congress has taken many strong stands on the war—uh—uh police action. We've requested that the President work out a peace settlement and bring our PW's home. It's all in the *Congressional Record*."

"But nothing's happened, things are getting worse. If the President can't stop the war, why doesn't Congress?"

"For a very simple reason, smart guy. The President probably knows something we don't know."

"Why doesn't he tell you what he knows?"

"Because if he told us, someone would probably leak it, and then the press would know and the American people would know. Do you want to have every Tom, Dick, and Harry in this country find out what the President knows about the war?"

"Dad, don't get mad, but the kids at school say Congress is impotent. They say you're all a bunch of eunuchs, and the President can do anything he wants because you're afraid of him."

"Well, you can tell the kids at school they don't know what the hell they're talking about. Why, we were talking about how to get out of this war when they were in kindergarten. It's very fashionable these days to complain that the President hasn't found a peaceful solution to the Vietnamese conflict. But he's only been at it four years, and you've got to give him a chance. If at the end of his second term in office he hasn't come up with a solution, then Congress will take decisive action.

"Great, Dad! Wait till I tell the guys at school!"

NO MORE BOMBS

It was hard to believe, but in October, 1972, the United States ran out of bombs.

Secretary of Defense Melvin Laird broke the bad news to President Nixon. "I'm sorry, Mr. President, but we have no bombs left to drop on Vietnam. We're completely out."

"But that's impossible," the President said. "I was assured we had enough bombs stockpiled for five years."

"Under ordinary conditions we would have, but we've been dropping them at such an accelerated rate that we ran out last Friday. There's isn't one bomb left in the United States or at any of its overseas bases."

"Can't we borrow some bombs from our allies?"

"We've already borrowed every bomb we could from Britain, France, Belgium, West Germany, Spain, and Greece. We owe them 2.42 billion bombs, and they say they aren't going to lend us any more until we pay the interest on the ones we have already. At six percent that comes to an awful lot of bombs."

"But, Melvin, we've got to have bombs, or our strategy of bringing Hanoi to her knees will fail. Surely a great industrial giant like the United States can rise to the challenge."

"We've tried, sir, but production just can't keep up with demand. Every time a bomb comes off the assembly line, it's immediately attached to a bomb rack and dropped on Vietnam. To make matters worse, the Air Force, Navy, and Marines are fighting over every bomb that is made. They had a dogfight over the Lockheed plant in San Diego the other morning, and the Navy shot down an Air Force B-52 because it claimed the Air Force had stolen their bomb."

"This is serious, Melvin. If we slow down the tempo of the bombing, the North Vietnamese will interpret it as a sign of weakness. Have you checked any of the underdeveloped countries? Surely they must have some we can buy."

"We've looked into it, Mr. President, but the underdeveloped countries are refusing to sell their bombs. They've decided bombs are more valuable than gold, and because of the shortage, they are now using them as currency. The latest rate of exchange is one hundred trucks for one bomb."

"How did we get into such a position?" the President asked in an exasperated voice.

"I guess it was our fault, Mr. President. When we said we would bomb only military targets in Vietnam, we had a sufficient supply of bombs. But when you gave the order to bomb anything they wanted to, the Air Force and Navy went ape.

"Also, the South Vietnamese army didn't help much. Every time they saw a water buffalo in a rice paddy, they called for an air strike. One sniper in a tree cost us two hundred thousand tons of bombs. We dropped more bombs on Highway One last week than we dropped in all of World War Two."

"I'm going to issue an executive order declaring that every dairy in the United States must start manufacturing bombs."

"Every dairy?" the Secretary of Defense said.

"That's correct. It's obvious my butter-and-bomb policy isn't working. So until we have enough bombs to halt Communist aggression, no one in this country gets any butter."

"That's a drastic measure in an election year, Mr. President."

"It has to be done, Melvin. I'm not going to be the first President of the United States to go down in history as the one who ran out of bombs."

FOR EYES ONLY

In dealing with the question of whether the New York *Times* was correct in printing excerpts from the top-secret Pentagon report as to how we got involved in Vietnam, one must understand the entire question of classifying government documents.

To begin with, all branches of the government classify documents. The more classified documents a department has in its files, the more important it considers the work it is doing.

The lowest government classification for a classified document is LOU, which stands for Limited Official Use. This classification could be stamped on a document to announce a softball game, an office party, the vacation schedule of department heads or what one must do in case of a nuclear bombing attack. (After the attack, report to your nearest post office and wait for instructions.) Almost anyone in the government family has access to LOU's, and you'll usually find mail-room boys reading them on elevators between deliveries of interoffice mail.

The next designation is CONFIDENTIAL, which is really between LOU and SECRET. CONFIDENTIAL could have some security information in it (for example, not only would it give the time of the softball game, but who was pitching for the other side). Fewer people are allowed to see a CONFIDENTIAL memo than a LOU. (In the case of a nuclear bombing attack, a CONFIDENTIAL memo might tell you what to do if the post office wasn't there.)

After CONFIDENTIAL comes SECRET. A SECRET document is so categorized on a N to K basis (Need to Know). Only those people who are actually involved in the project are supposed to have access to SECRET documents. They have an urgency to them that demands: "Deal with this before coffee break."

The next classification is TOP SECRET. It's hard for someone in the government to tell the difference between SECRET and TOP SECRET, other than when reading a TOP SECRET message your palms sweat more.

The final classification is LIM DIS, standing for Limited Distribution. A LIM DIS is TOP SECRET with hair on it. The highest classification known publicly is LIM DIS FEO (For Eyes Only). If you get one of those, it means you were in some way responsible for the nuclear attack. (See paragraph 3 of this article.)

Now the important thing to understand is why people in the

government classify their documents. Here is a scientific breakdown of reasons and percentages. The reasons a paper is classified are:

1. To make the person who wrote the document look important—10 percent.

2. To make the person reading the document think he is more important than he really is—10 percent.

3. To keep secretaries and file clerks busy during slack periods—15 percent.

4. To be on record in case someone ever calls you on a mistake someone else in the department made—10 percent.

5. To make sure the press will take it seriously when the document is leaked to them—15 percent.

6. To impress the public with your frankness when you declassify it—10 percent.

7. To protect the person (or persons) who were responsible for making the mistake (s)—25 percent.

8. National security—5 percent.

What one must always keep in mind when dealing with something as dicey as the McNamara Pentagon report is that it may taste like national security to some people, but others say it's spinach and the hell with it.